Inspirations ᴑʏ ʟɪfe in Faith
Volume 1

"It all starts with faith which is the size of a mastered seed".

Nomusa Buleni

Nomusa Buleni

About Nomusa Buleni

Nomusa (Myeza) Buleni was born and raised in South Africa where she studied for a degree in nursing at University of Zululand. She is a well to do woman and a hard worker. Nomusa is an ordained church Elder and in many years in her walk with the Lord have grown an aptitude into Christian Counseling and a sound medical practitioner trainer with an undivided passion to serve. She is a veritable teacher of the word of God with true marks of a sound leader and today she heads major female conventions and organizations. Nomusa have through all hardships has managed to raise 3 daughters and a son and is an awesome grandmother. At the time of writing her first book Nomusa had travelled across Africa and Europe teaching and preaching in church conferences, training and leadership seminars. The Lord has blessed this resilient woman of God in service and ministry to the less fortunate where she have mothered dozens ranging from young people to adults and she is spiritual mother both to pastors and bishops both in Africa and Europe where she now a British citizen where the Lord called her to sojourn similarly as he did to our father of faith Abraham. With the step of believing God she kept going as per the leading of God until the inception of this project. Among her favorites quotations from this book is "*Be inspired so that you can inspire*" as you get blessed with this mental liberating book. She is a born again and spirit filled vibrant and inspirational motivator; may the Lord bless you and move you to another realm as you read this book. Without faith and obedience to the voice of the Lord this book would not have been here.

Hebrews 11:6.

Nomusa Buleni

Published by AuthorHouse   05/27/2015

Published by Nomusa Buleni   10/24/2016

ISBN: 978-1-5049-4265-2 (sc)
ISBN: 978-1-5049-4266-9 (e)

Library of Congress Control Number: 2015907747

authorHOUSE®

AuthorHouse™ UK
1663 Liberty Drive Bloomington,
IN 47403 USA
www.authorhouse.co.uk
Phone: 0800.197.4150

Nomusa Buleni

Print information available on the last page.

Dedication

This project would not have come out smoothly and soundly without the support and prayers of my loving daughter Thembeka and her husband. She gave me a push until I met my publisher. At one point, as a mom, I found myself busy and thought, Let me put aside the writing of this series, but with your unwavering support, here we are today. It's always good to have you, Anele, my dear daughter, when you would sit on my computer and help. Life events are smooth and easy when you have the right people with right attitude around who can relate to your burden, visions, and calling. The most amazing thing with a burden is that it will not easily go away until you respond positively to it. The writing of this book has brought me closer to my son, Ndabezinhle, who has been the greatest instrument in the production of this work. I say thank you, my son. If you are a parent, you should always allow your children to look at and be involved in your work. Mothers, be inspired in working together as family. A certain aspect of relationship is brought by working, and it is the only moment you can tell the talents in your children and family members. I did then discover that my youngest daughter, Sinethemba, has an amazing gift of analysis and perfection in her. She would proofread and make corrections to my work. I love you and thank you for hard work. Special dedication and love goes to all my grandchildren. I also dedicate this book to

Bishop Rupare, whom I hold in high esteem, and my pastors, church, and friends who prayed and supported me throughout. God bless you. I thank you, the reader, because this book was designed by the Holy Spirit with you in mind. To all, may the joy and love of our Lord Jesus Christ fill your hearts. Amen.

Table of Contents

Preface

Knowledge of the truth found solely in God's Word gives and yields faith. Faith is believing in something based on the promptings of the Spirit of God, thus requiring something to believe in. The New-Age movement believes that we can believe things into existence, which is not the same kind of faith we believers should have or dwell on. Our faith is based upon the truth in God's Word. Therefore, knowing what God's Word has to say about something gives us the ability to believe it. Putting Christ as the basis of our faith will eventually yield results. Our faith should be based upon God's Word. Inspirations of Life in Faith is a compilation of models that build a strong base for a Christian life. As that happens, there is evidence of fruits and personal growth in Christ, the hope of glory. For example, how can you have faith to pray for healing, believing that God will heal you, if you don't know that it was God's will for you to heal? I have this to say to you, brethren:

In Isaiah 53: 5, the Bible teaches us that "but he (Jesus) was wounded for our transgressions (sins and unholy walk), he was bruised for our iniquities: the chastisement (payment) of our peace was upon him; and with his stripes we are healed." The scripture here is telling us that we are healed by God through Jesus's suffering, meaning that it was then God's will to heal us. Moreover, He had us in His will. It leaves no room for any one of us to say that if God wants, He will heal us, but it's something that God has done already. This takes away ownership of disease when we say that this is my sickness.

This is why Satan works so hard to tell the church that it may not be God's will for them to be healed. Why? It casts doubt, the opposite of faith, upon the hearts of God's children. (Where there is no doubt, it's hard for the Devil to function.) Furthermore, how can we receive the promises of God if we don't know what they are? We must first know the truth (God always operates in truth) and then believe it. That is biblical faith. In Mark 9: 23, Jesus tells the man that he has to believe that all things are possible.

We have to believe and trust the Word of God. Jesus told His disciples that all things (referring to the promises of God) are possible for those who trust God. You cannot have a successful Christian life without fully trusting in Jesus. How can you believe something that nobody told you? You cannot. It is important to know what the Word of God is and has said and is saying so that we can believe it. Faith comes by hearing God's Word: "So then faith cometh by hearing, and hearing by the word of God" (Romans 10: 17). I pray that this publication will not only minister to you but also inspire you to new heights in your walk with the Lord. Amen.

With   Love,
Nomusa Buleni

Introduction

The reason for this book is to inspire and edify you, the reader, to a simpler understanding and bring you to the knowledge of different ways of dealing with daily events in your Christian walk. Unless something is done and taught, Christian life may remain an ambiguous subject with few people knowing their position in regards to Christ. The Holy Spirit has been at work teaching and leading us into a simpler defined pattern of how to deal with self by way of self-positioning in the body of Christ. The Holy Spirit does not possess us, but He rather gently seeks and awaits our desiring of Him. He nudges us and yearns for us to allow Him to lead us in the will of God.

We must learn to hear His voice and then obey it. Following His lead is a remarkable adventure. Serving him is the best experience you can ever have because the experience itself brings about maturity. The more we follow God's leading, the more He qualifies us. The church of today has many gifts and talents, some of which are known and utilized. Others have been stolen and abused by the Devil. The Holy Spirit has put these gifts, which are heavenly treasures, into us, the earthly vessels, for the good of the body of Christ. Understanding and identifying them is vital and important. The spiritual gift that has not been identified or used cannot benefit anyone. The truth you have not known can never set you free, though the Bible teaches that the truth sets you free.

This truth is like food that is good for body building. You have to eat food to build your body. The aim of this book is to carry you to a climax of revelation, inspiration, and grounding in faith. This book brings you in ways in which you can gain a better understanding of who you are – in other words, your position in Christ. When I met most of the Christians I know – though it is true that when I looked at them, they clearly love God – there is nothing to inspire them. The fire in them will easily die down. There were two men, Timothy and Titus. These men were spiritually fathered by Paul, but with a closer look at them, we can note a lot of differences. Even their names can give us a clue as to their differences. Titus is tight, and Timothy is very timid man.

Timothy cannot do much in his ministry and calling without having encouragement and inspiration from his spiritual father, Paul. Look at how Paul talks to Timothy: "My son do the work of the evangelist", "shake the gift that is in you", "study to show thyself a workman," "pray and exercise thy faith", and "I have fought a good fight of faith." Timothy needs this inspiration. On the contrary, Titus is okay without inspiration. He does not need anyone to push him; he can do well on his own. Readers, I want you to be inspired as you read this book. Learn about the character of the people you lead and treat them well in wisdom. Identify and nurture spiritual gifts within your congregants. Moreover, cause your congregants to be hungry for righteousness so that our good master will feed them.

Matthew 5 tells us that blessed are those who hunger for righteousness, for they shall be filled.

As we shall see and learn throughout this book, certain truths are to remain like the tongue that shapes us. You can never know a person until he opens his mouth to talk. We are who we are because of what we say. God created the world we live in by simply speaking it into existence. All he had to say was "Let there be this and that," and it was so. The huge lesson here is that you can create your own world by speaking positively. Likewise, you can destroy a lot of good things by negative confession. The truth of the matter is that your tongue has power. Most of the biblical characters and their lifestyles were recorded so that we can be inspired to seek more and do better in our walk with the Lord. This book has been simplified so as to transmit life inspirations at a level that is easy to comprehend. I pray that you will find it useful in your day-to-day walk as a child of God.

CHAPTER I

Christianity

The central tenet of Christianity is the belief in Jesus as the Son of God and the Messiah (Christ). This is the paramount thought and pillar of sound Christianity. We Christians believe that our Lord Jesus Christ is the Messiah, whom God anointed and is of God as the Saviour of entire humanity, and we hold that Jesus's coming was the fulfilment of messianic prophecies of the Old and New Testaments. The Christian concept of the Messiah differs significantly from the contemporary Jewish concept. The core Christian belief is that through belief in and acceptance of the death and resurrection of the Lord Jesus Christ, Son of God, sinful humans can be reconciled to God and are thereby offered salvation and the promise of eternal life, in which we derive unmerited goodness from God (grace).

Having said this, we need to note that there are various theological disputes over the nature of Jesus during the early centuries of Christian history. As Christians, we believe that Jesus is God incarnate and the "true God and true man" (or both fully divine and fully human). The Lord Jesus, having become fully human, suffered the pains and temptations of a mortal man, as He was human, but He did not sin. Again, as fully God, He was raised to life again by the power of the Holy Ghost. The Bible teaches that "God raised him from the dead," He ascended to heaven, and He is "seated at the right hand of the Father." He is alive for evermore and will ultimately return (Acts 1: 9–11).

To fulfil the messianic prophecy, such as the resurrection of the dead, the Last Judgment and final establishment of the kingdom of God, according to the gospels of Matthew and Luke, Jesus was conceived through the Holy Spirit and was born of the Virgin Mary. Not much of Jesus's boyhood is recorded in any of the gospels. In comparison, his adulthood, especially when we look at the week before His death, is well-documented. That part of His life was and is believed to be crucial. The biblical accounts of Jesus's ministry include His early boyhood, baptism, miracles, preaching, teaching, deeds, and social and prayer life. Jesus came and taught that His coming was so that we might have life in full (John 10: 10).

We can by no means have Christians without Jesus Christ or the gift of eternal life that is found only in Him. Christianity is not just a religion. It is the life given to us by God and revealed through Jesus. God found His dwelling in the hearts of men who have received the Lord Jesus as their Saviour.

John 1: 1: "in the beginning was the Word, and the Word was with God, and the Word was God."

John 1: 12: "but as many as received him, to them gave he power to become the sons of God, even to them that believe on his name." John 1: 14: "And the Word was made flesh, and dwelt among us, (and we beheld his

glory, the glory as of the only begotten of the Father,) full of grace and truth."

In John 1: 1 and 1: 14, Jesus gives us a chance to allow Him and His Father to come and dwell in us.

Revelation 3: 20–21 says that a dynamic change will take place in our lives when we open up to Him.

As described by Paul in one of his pastoral epistles: "Therefore if any man be in Christ, he is a new creature: old things are passed away; behold all things are become new" (2 Corinthians 5: 17).

The making of us who were gentiles to be saints and children of God is confirmed here in Colossians 1: 26–27 by the apostle Paul as a mystery, "even the mystery which hath been hid from ages and from generations, but now is made manifest to his saints (us now who have received His Son): to whom God would make known what is the riches of the glory of this mystery among the Gentiles; which is Christ in you, the hope of glory."

Who Are We Really? Our Identity in Christ

Most importantly, if we delay or fail to realize or receive who we are in Christ, our faith will be crippled and null. If you feel unworthy to exercise your authority and right in Christ, you will not be doing it in the fullness of faith and will lack assurance. The truth is that we, by our own power and effort, are unworthy, but it is the blood of Christ that makes us worthy. If we say we are unable and unworthy when the blood says we are, we are denying the work that Christ did for us on the cross at Calvary. This is an elementary subject that most Christians do not fully comprehend. However, it remains a powerful foundation to spiritual breakthrough for those who understand it. You are not an ordinary forgiven sinner. Search for these things in the Word of God, and know the truth. Jesus said clearly that if we continue in His Word, we will know the truth and the truth will set us free: "And ye shall know the truth, and the truth shall make you free." (John 8: 32).

The opposite of truth is deception or false beliefs (apostasy), and this subject is no exception. If you see yourself as a failure, you will not be able to boldly exercise your authority in Christ because you will feel unworthy (even after the blood of Christ has made you worthy [Proverbs 23: 7]). You cannot live a positive life with a negative mindset.

You are never what you do not perceive yourself as. Furthermore, after we have accepted the free gift of salvation through faith in the shed blood of the Lord Jesus Christ and as we grow and mature in the Lord (your continuing sanctification), we will begin to notice some changes in how we conduct ourselves, behave, and think. In most cases, you will realize that your heart for God (soul) grows more and more in agreement with God and His law (which is the spiritual Word of God), but your flesh will still want to go back to the old ways of living. All true born-again Christians have a split personality (so to speak). When you walk not in sin (you stay saved), sin may lay along your path as a trap as you grow in your Christian walk with the Lord. However, there is a covering of God's grace to overcome and protect you. Philippians 2: 12 says, "The flesh is very responsive to sinful edges because of the sinful nature that we were born in."

Romans 7: 21–25 says, "I find then a law, that, when I would do good, evil is present with me. For I delight in the law of God after the inward man: But I see another law in my members, warring against the law of my mind, and bringing me into captivity to the law of sin which is in my members. O wretched man that I am! Who shall deliver me from the body of this death? I thank God through Jesus Christ our Lord. So then with the mind I my self serve the law of God; but with the flesh the law of sin."

We learn and understand this true teaching that though the soul is saved, your flesh and present physical body is still dead and cannot be salvaged. It will perish and return to the earth. (You will get a new glorified body at the return of Christ Jesus.) Your present flesh will still lust to do those things that are spiritually unlawful, while at the same time, your heart and the Spirit will condemn those thoughts and feelings and empower you to avoid the temptation. No Christian is perfect in the flesh, though, and as you go through this life, you will sometimes give in to those feelings and will sin in the flesh (1 Corinthians 9: 27).

God's Nature

When we look into the nature of God's existence, it is evident that God exists in Himself. This is an ultimate self-governing cause whereby there is no need for human ideology or help. He is a self-attuning God who leaves and exists outside nature's influence and is not bound the laws of nature, in which He is the creator.

He loves nature and mankind. That's why He created them. His love for nature and humanity is not based on the creation's merits, but rather on His own pleasure and for His own glory (Colossians 1: 16 and Revelation 4: 11).

You are loved by God, not because of what you have done, but because of who you are. You were created in His image, which literally translate as "function." The word "image" here does not speak of physical appearance or likeness. Instead, it means "function" or operational "likenesses" (Genesis 1: 27). It brings out an operational likeness or functioning in like manner with God that gives Him pleasure and thereby glory. His love for us is so profound and deep.

He later proved this love through His only begotten son Jesus. At no time, place, situation, or condition has He stopped expressing the unconditional love for us and His created nature. Failing to receive and realize this ultimate love disqualifies us from being filled with the holy fullness of His Godly nature of love. We will lack His fullness in our lives until we come to know of His deep love toward us (Ephesians 4: 13 and Ephesians 3: 17–19).

We have been blinded by religion. Religion is merely a human effort to please and serve God with ignorance of his grace (unmerited goodness of God). As a result, many people have misinterpreted the word and laws of God, and as a result, came into apostasy. This has resulted in not only the falling away from the sound doctrine of God but also paving the way for the enemy who has taken the occasion to completely drag many souls from grace. This a terrible loss we are battling with in the kingdom of God. We are winning this war by passing on the love and merciful nature of God.

God never wanted people to be under the law. His sweet nature was to allow us be independent and enjoy freedom of free choosing. Jesus brought us freedom and truth (John 1: 17), and Jesus Christ was the redemptive tool to lead man out of the curse of the law (Galatians 4: 5 and Hebrews 2: 15).

Without Jesus Christ, it's difficult to understand the extent of God's nature, love, and being – even why we are created. He taught and simplified things for those who would follow Him and His teachings. He is the fulfilment of the law, not the breaker of it. It is fundamental that we come to the knowledge of Christ be revelation. On the contrary, trying to understand Him and His teachings with the carnal mind might be critically misleading if not perceive Him as another law breaker and sinner. Revelation is essential through the help and leading of the Holy Spirit.

Grace makes life easy for all. Whether you are born again or not, life is no longer the same as it was before grace.

The sweetness of life under grace is incomparable to life lived before the death of Jesus Christ when communities where dominated by the strict laws and domination by the super imperatorial rulers of the age. It's human nature to forget to acknowledge God when all is well. Otherwise, it goes to the extent of questioning the existence of this merciful creator as if He does not exists.

Man has been a habitual sinner here on earth, firstly in forgetting his main reasons for being on earth. At times, people sin, and God remains quiet and seems unmoved by man's horrific standards. Psalm 50: 22 says that every sin done has a payday, and it is not a good payday either. People feel cushy in the shadows of religion that have set standards for pleasing God, forgetting that the only way and the only truth and life that will lead us all to eternity. Through Jesus, we have peace with God and Him (Jesus) alone (Romans 5: 1).

The coming of Jesus was not to authorize other new strange laws or remove all that was there. The laws were a pointer to He who was to come, not a distracter. If we fail to understand the intentions of the law, we also fail to understand the trinity and what we have to do to please our Creator. In principle, the law reveals (Romans 7: 7 and 7: 25):

- Sin, death, and eternal condemnation
- God's nature
- The position of man
- The position of the Devil and what he does

The aim of God is to track us back to the original fellowship and relationship we once had with Him. In other words, it is there to restore the original plane of God. In revealing all this, God wants us to see ourselves in the position of sin and end our natural endeavours in reaching out to Him with our own efforts. In His holiness, all man's efforts are temporal and still fail to cover sin until He comes down to the rescue of us all. Religion did not receive Jesus as the solution to the prevailing problem but rather as another problem. To sum it up, can God in His almighty send a problem on top of another problem? Obviously not – He wouldn't do that. The laws were never meant to harm humanity, and neither was Jesus there to freely break it because He was the Son of God.

God send His son to come for our rescue in the same likeness of the sinful nature to buy us back to Him (God), and we see Jesus suffering dearly to carry out this agonizing task. Jesus was a practical teacher and a great imitator of God on earth but in all holiness. The price was higher, so there needed to be someone who was equally higher to free us.

Great teachings are drawn from the stories of Jesus's parables of us coming back to our Father. In that alone, we derive the supernatural nature of God.

- The parable of the prodigal son (Luke 15: 11–32)
- God being Christ reconciling the world to Himself (2 Corinthians 5: 19)

- The parable of unmerciful servant (Matthew 18: 21–35)
- The parable of the lost coin (Luke 15: 8–10)

You Were Purchased at a Steep Price

The wages of sin are death, but Jesus paid that price for you and me so that we would become His special people and a holy nation. God's Word tells us that we were purchased by the precious blood of the lamb: "For ye are bought with a price: therefore glorify God in your body, and in your spirit, which are God's" (1 Corinthians 6: 20). Why did Jesus purchase us with His own blood? It was because of His deep love for us, and He deeply desires to have a loving relationship with you and me (Romans 5: 8).

God did not send an angel to die for us on the cross simply because of the fate of the sin. An angel would have been even lower in rank with Lucifer the fallen angel, and this work of total redemption needed a superior being both in authority and power to do complete work. If you have repented your sins and accepted the gift of God, referring to the forgiveness of sins through the blood of Jesus, God's Word tells us that we receive justification (Galatians 2: 16). If any person is justified, it means they are made innocent or made just as if they did not sin in the first place. However, our sins have been put away, deleted, and removed. It has also been decided not to bring them into account anymore. This is all a result of the death of Jesus on the cross. Now we are justified – made perfect and whole again, that is – and made right with God. We are entitled to a clean and undefiled conscience and commanded to live a holy life acceptable to God.

Romans 12: 1 says that if you are still beating yourself up over your past failures that have been nailed to the cross, you are denying the work that Christ has done for you. When your past deeds begin to come back into your mind, just remind yourself that you are forgiven and that God no longer counts your past faults and wrongs. It is just a trick of the Devil to derail you back into sinful life. Resist him, and he will flee from you. A clean conscience before the Lord agrees with what Christ has done in removing your sins and declaring you as justified or innocent before Jesus Christ.

The truth of the matter is that our sins have not simply been covered. Rather, they have actually been removed from our account. This was not possible in the Old Testament, but by the blood of Jesus, the removal of sins is now a living a reality (John 1: 29 and Matthew 26: 28).

If forgiving us was not enough, God Himself chose to forget our failures for His own sake. When He sees us, He doesn't want to remember our failures. He wants to see you as His chosen child who stands blameless before Him:

- "and their sins and iniquities will I remember no more"
  (Hebrews 10: 17).
- "blessed is the one whose sin the Lord will never count against them" (Romans 4: 8).

My friend, God does not hold anything against us anymore. We are free because Romans 8: 2 – the law of the spirit – has set us free. We should rejoice at this great announcement.

We Have Peace with God

We have been justified (this is an act of God's removal of the guilt and penalty of sin from a sinner while at the same time declaring the sinner righteous through Christ's atoning sacrifice) and made right with God. Therefore, we have peace with God. This means that your relationship with God has been restored and that you can boldly enter His presence with a clean conscience because of your faith in Christ Jesus and the work that He has done for us on the cross.

Romans 5: 1 says, "Therefore being justified by faith, we have peace with God through our Lord Jesus Christ."

As a result of your having been forgiven and pardoned in Christ, a great exchange has taken place. One of the things is our sin for Jesus's own righteousness. Let us observe this through a few scriptures: Romans 3: 22, 3: 25, and 5: 17. Jesus received what we deserved (punishment for our sins), and He gave us His righteousness in exchange. This is how God showed us His great love and compassion. In the same manner, Jesus was being obedient to God the Father. It is a great mystery indeed.

"Forgiven Sinner or Saint?"

Unless your sins have been washed away, you remain a sinner. Here, your status, creed, colour, gender, location, economic status, education, or fame do not earn you the privilege. Unless you are saved, you cannot be a saint. The day you accepted Jesus as your Lord and Saviour and believe in Him, you became a new creation in Christ. This newly created person is in righteousness and true holiness: We are not just born again, but we have also become sons and daughters of God, jointed with the Son (Romans 8: 17 and John 1: 12–13). "co-heirs of the kingdom with His Son." So what happened to the old you? The old you was crucified with Christ. God did not repair the old you. He created a new you in Christ, which is what the Bible refers to when talking about being born again.

"Jesus answered, Verily, verily, I say unto thee, except a man be born of water and of the Spirit, he cannot enter into the kingdom of God. That which is born of the flesh is flesh; and that which is born of the Spirit is spirit. Marvel not that I said unto thee, Ye must be born again." (John 3: 5–7).

Galatians 2: 20 says that this is referring to our spirits, not our souls. Soon, we will look and learn more about the difference between your spirit and soul.

You are Seated with Christ, A Position of Authority

Many Christians do not realize what this means. To be seated refers to a place of authority. Jesus is seated at the right hand of God, and God's Word tells us that we are seated with Christ. Because of our position and our sitting in Christ, we are positioned in a place of authority over all sickness, diseases, and demons. Jesus said that signs and wonders, including casting out demons (which requires authority [Mark 16: 17–20]), would follow those who believe. We did not earn this right. Instead, it was accorded to us through grace and salvation.

Revelation 5: 9–10 says, "or thou wast slain, and hast redeemed us to God by thy blood out of every kindred, and tongue, and people, and nation; and hast made us unto our God kings and priests: and we shall reign on the earth."

The truth is that we can speak with authority over that sickness and command evil spirits to flee away from your body and life in Jesus's name (Philippians 2: 9–11).

We can command those limbs to grow because we have authority and delegated power from Lord Jesus. This was the standard practice in the early church when the followers of Christ were healing the sick, delivering the demon-possessed, and raising the dead. The same is true when it comes to demons. We do not need to ask God to remove the demons, but instead, we take up the authority Christ has given us and exercise it through faith using Jesus's name to exorcize the devils. Remember that the only reference to prayer for healing in the New Testament is found in James 5: 15.

The rest of the New Testament scriptures tell us of how Jesus, His disciples, and the early church would exercise their faith when they went forth to heal the sick and deliver the oppressed. They were not asking the Father to heal the sick. They were saying things like, "Be healed in Jesus's name" or "Rise and walk." Jesus taught and made it clear that we have authority here on earth, which is naturally ours through our position in being seated with Christ. He demonstrated this when he cursed the fig tree.

"Who is God?"

Who is God? What is God? How can we know God?

Do we really know who our God is? I would like to begin by teaching about who God is to us, and eventually, I will leave you to do a personal examination on assessing your need for a relationship with Him. and I believe at the end of this part of the series, we will all come to the full understanding of who we have believed in Him, trusted, and (at times) failed to understand. We will also endeavour to separate His acts and true identity. There is a vast difference between what God does (His acts) and who He really is. I have also come to understand that many people want God and have slight knowledge of who He is but refuse the way to the God who they profess and acknowledge. This is the Lord Jesus for simple reasons that we shall see. Have you observed this truth that most people in the universe talk and accept

God as creator of the universe, but not many want or accept Jesus as God's Son sent by the God they accept?

The Fact

It is a common element that all religions agree that there is a creator somewhere, though little is known about this deity, and few efforts have been made to seek more about Him. Even fewer have rejected Jesus but agree on the existence of God and His ultimate power over creation. The fact of God's existence is so conspicuous, both through creation and through man's conscience. Accordingly, the Bible never attempts to prove the existence of God; rather, it assumes His existence from the very beginning (Genesis 1: 1). What the Bible does is reveal the nature, character, work, and acts of God and what He says about Himself in terms of identity.

The Definition

Thinking correctly and positively about God is of utmost importance because a false idea about God is idolatry. Thinking outside Him will not leave us free of guilt. To start with, a good summary definition of God is the supreme being; the creator and ruler of all that is; and the self-existent one who is perfect in power, goodness, wisdom, majesty, and holiness.

His Nature

We know the things that are true of God for one among many given reasons: In His mercy, He has condescended to reveal some of His qualities to us. God is spirit and resides in truth by nature intangible. "God is a Spirit: and they that worship him must worship him in spirit and in truth" (John 4: 24).

God is one, but He exists as three: God the Father, God the Son, and God the Holy Spirit (Matthew 3: 16–17). Also, we see we are likened to God's true nature as we are a composition of body, soul, and spirit. Hence, our worship is done in three forms: spirit, truth, and faith. God is infinite and never-ending (1 Timothy 1: 17). Amen.

Incomparable cannot be compared to anything. He is too holy (2 Samuel 7: 22) and unchanging. Malachi 3: 6 says, "For I am the Lord, I change not; therefore ye sons of Jacob are not consumed."

"God is not a man that he should lie; neither the son of man that he should repent: hath he said, and shall he not do it? or hath he spoken, and shall he not make it good?" (Numbers 23: 19). God exists everywhere (Psalm 139: 7–12), knows everything (Psalm 147: 5 and Isaiah 40: 28), and has all power and authority (Revelation 19: 6).

His Character

Here are some of God's characteristics as revealed in the Bible: God is just (Acts 17: 31); loving (Ephesians 2: 4–5); trustworthy, just, and truthful (John 14: 6); and holy (1 John 1: 5). God shows compassion (2 Corinthians 1: 3), mercy (Romans 9: 15), and grace (Romans 5: 17). God judges sin (Psalm 5: 5), but also offers forgiveness (Psalm 130: 4). He is all to all and all in all but never changing.

His Work

We cannot understand God fully apart from His deeds, because what God does flows from who He is. Here is a list of God's works, past, present, and future:

- Creator: He created the world (Genesis 1: 1 and Isaiah 42: 5).
- Sustains: He actively sustains the world (Colossians 1: 17).
- Self-directing: He is executing His eternal plan (Ephesians 1: 11), which involves the redemption of man from the curse of sin and death (Galatians 3: 13–14).
- Guiding: He draws people to Christ (John 6: 44).
- Fatherhood: He disciplines His children (Hebrews 12: 6).
- Majestic: He will judge the world (Revelation 20: 11–15) through the word.

A Relationship with Him

A relationship with Him is all humanity needs, but there is a way to obtain this. In the Son, God became incarnate (John 1: 14). The Son of God became the Son of Man and is therefore the bridge between God and man (John 14: 6). 1 Timothy 2: 5 says "For there is one God and one Mediator between God and men, the Man Christ Jesus." It is only through the Son that we have forgiveness of sins (Ephesians 1: 7).

John 15: 15 discusses reconciliation with God, while Romans 5: 10 covers eternal salvation.

2 Timothy 2: 10 says that in Jesus Christ, "all the fullness of the Deity lives in bodily form." Colossians 1: 15 says "who is the image of the invisible God, the firstborn of every creature."

The Names of God

Ø El Shaddai means God Almighty (Genesis 17: 1). "God Almighty - El Shaddai, the God - proved sufficient for everything. The wonderful El Shaddai (the power to create new things from nothing with need no help, assistance, or ideas) runs through the entire kingdom of grace."

Ø Elohim means God the creator (Genesis 1: 1). A beautiful trait or symbol of Elohim is that he never lies. It is impossible for God to lie (Numbers 23: 19). This is the only thing that God fails to do in His entire nature. Elohim thundered to Israel, "I am the Lord your Elohim. ... (God) ... You shall have no other gods before me" (Exodus 20: 2–3). Moses, the servant and amazing prophet of the God who does not lie, encouraged the Israelites to "acknowledge and take to heart this day that the Lord is Elohim in heaven above and on the earth below. There is no other gods before Him, He alone is God" (Deuteronomy 4: 39).

Ø El Elyon means the most High God (Genesis 14: 18). "El Elyon" derives its compound meaning (translated "God Most High" or "Most High God"). It then occurs approximately twelve times in the Old Testament. It occurs four times in Genesis 14: 18–20,

22. Melchizedek, king of Salem, brought forth bread and wine to celebrate Abram's military victory. We are again told that Melchizedek was a priest of God Most High. He blessed Abraham and said, "Blessed be Abram of God Most High who possesses heaven and earth, and blessed be God Most High, who has delivered your enemies into your hand." We are told that Abram then gave Melchizedek a tenth of all (tithing). Later, Abram is said to have told the king of Sodom that he (Abraham) lifted up his hand to Yahweh, God Most High (El Elyon), possessor of heaven and earth. This means that Abraham worshiped the Most High God.

Ø El-Olam means everlasting God (Genesis 21: 33). El-Olam is everlasting God and is a secret name for God, pointing at God's mysterious nature. In the prefix El is derived from the title Elohim ("strong Creator"). Olam means time or age. In ancient Hebrew, rabbis spelled it "alam," denoting "hidden," bringing out the mysterious nature of God. God's everlasting or timeless nature – without beginning or end – is one of the most profound mysteries of His nature … as in being the same yesterday, today and forever.

Ø El-Kana meaning jealous or zealous (Exodus 20: 5). The Lord of hosts and the related names, Lord God of hosts and God of hosts (1 Samuel), make this title more frequent compound title for God in the Old Testament.

Ø Jehovah Mekoddishkem meaning the Lord who sanctifies (Exodus 31: 13) (yeh-ho-vaw' M-qadash). This means the Lord who sanctifies you or the Lord who makes you Holy. In the Old Testament, Jehovah Mekoddishkem appears only twice. Jehovah Mekoddishkem in the Septuagint is "kurios ho hagiazôn humas" or the Lord that sanctifies you. When translated, it is the existing one or Lord.

THE PREEMINENCE OF GOD

The Bible portrays God as preeminent in every way, all the time, and in every situation. God is set apart from all other living beings. One would expect the creator to have pre-eminence in a relationship to that which is created. Never should we mix Him with creation. Note that He was not created like we all were. Moreover, we are the work of His hands (Ephesians 2: 10). This unique preeminent position that God holds can be seen in the following diverse ways.

PREEMINENT AS CREATOR OVER ALL THINGS

No one can doubt or question the pre-eminence of one who alone possesses immortality and has the ability to give and sustain life at His will. The Word of God describe in these terms and promises that God is worthy of honour, glory, and eternal dominion because of it (Acts 17: 24–25). Regardless of whether we are aware or we like it or we don't, the fact remains that He is the creator (1 Timothy 6: 13–16).

"Worthy art Thou, our Lord and our God to receive glory and honor and power; for Thou didst create all things and because of Thy will they existed, and were created" (Revelation 4: 11).

PREEMINENT AS SOVEREIGN RULER

1 Timothy 6: 15: It recognizes God's preeminent position as the sovereign ruler over creation, the work of His hands. The Sovereign God rules everywhere both in the firmament and on earth among the dead and the living and over all creation. It take grace to see this great mystery.

Psalm 47: 8 ("God reigneth over the heathen: God sitteth upon the throne of his holiness"), Psalm 62: 11, 93: 1–2, and 97: 1–2: We can recognize in Psalms that some important aspects of God's sovereign rule are emphasized and exposed. We then learn that God's reign is everlasting and is expressed in characterization by His majesty, strength, and power along with the fact that righteousness and justice are the foundation of His throne now and forevermore. It is also because of this reason that we are encouraged to rejoice and expect that the day of the Lord will come and that He will reign as king in the midst of mankind.

PREEMINENT AS THE ONLY TRUE GOD

The Bible is also consistent in describing God's pre-eminence as the only true God (Numbers 23: 19). Most people would therefore think suggest that God takes on many forms or can be known in and through many different paths. This element is nowhere near at peace with a scriptural view and in fact would be in direct opposition to it. The recorded Lord's Prayer teaches us that God our Father recognized only one true God (John 17: 1–3). During the apostolic age, they taught about the pre-eminent nature of God when they referred to Him as the only God. There are two examples as found in the letter of Paul to Timothy and in the letter to Jude:

1 Timothy 1: 17: "Now unto the King eternal, immortal, invisible, the only wise God, be honor and glory for ever and ever. Amen."

Jude 1: 24–25: "God through the prophet Isaiah declares Himself the only true God calling all men to turn to Him for salvation."

Isaiah 45: 22–23: "look unto me, and be ye saved, all the ends of the earth: for I am God, and there is none else. I have sworn by myself, the word is gone out of my mouth in righteousness, and shall not return, that unto me every knee shall bow, every tongue shall swear." Isaiah 46: 9–10

God Is Sovereign

This means supreme ruler, especially a monarch. This is an absolute emperor ruler, monarch, supreme ruler, or potentate who is independent, self-governing, self-determining, self-legislating, and not aligned to anyone or anything.

1 Chronicles 29: 11–12: God is a sovereign ruler in and out of this entire universe. There is no higher authority over Him; neither can anyone to question Him. Our God possesses all power and ability; He is in absolute control

of everything, and all things are subject to His rule. He is all-powerful and all-knowing; no one can tell Him to do anything against His will. His will is perfect. He is present everywhere (omnipresent), so no one can hide from Him or escape His scrutiny, wrath, or presence. He is all-knowing, so there is nothing about which He is unaware. He remains a wise God. Nothing occurs without His divine permission. God commands the forces of nature and uses them to achieve His divine purpose and pleasure. He established laws that govern the entire cosmos, and only He can overrule their effect. Even His hosts can operate only within limits prescribed by God; they are very limited. God directs and gives charge to people, circumstances, and events. He removes kings and sets others on the throne.

We also see in Daniel 2: 21 that without God's providence, no one could spend the day. Job 12: 10 says, "In whose hand is the soul of every living thing, and the breath of all mankind."

Proverbs 19: 21: In fact, difficulties and suffering are tools in God's sovereign hands with which He shapes you into the express image of the invisible God. The Bible tells us that Romans 8: 28: Our sovereign God is actively directing all things for the purposes that were predestined before time, but this is within the context of His master plan. He gives all of us the freedom to choose how we will participate.

Jeremiah 10: 23: "O Lord, I know that the way of man is not in himself: it is not in man that walketh to direct his steps."

God Is Present Everywhere

Psalm 139: 7–10: Emanuel means God is with us. Because He is an infinite Spirit, He is not restricted to being in one location at any given time. He exists out of time because time is what he gave to process us. He fills every space throughout the entire earth with His personal attributes. Although God is different, all creation is the work of His hands. The entire creation exists within Him and for Him.

Acts 17: 28: "In Him we live and move and exist." We are all alive in His presence every moment of every day because there is life in its fullness in Him. There is no time when we are alone without Him; He watches what we do. It is also amazing to note that He does not adjudicate our choices. He is cool and always allows us to make our own choices. When we do something good that nobody else knows about, God knows, hears, watches, and sees it and will reward us accordingly. He also sees the bad things we do in secret (Hebrews 4: 13).

We actually have the presence of almighty God living inside us, and out of it, we gain light and insight.

1 Corinthians 3: 16: God needs us to consciously live wholly in His presence each day. His ever-presence makes it possible for us to be in constant communication with Him and to depend on Him in every situation as we enjoy true fellowship with Him. We often ignore the presence of God because we are so preoccupied with issues in our own lives. Sometimes, we even forget He is with us while we are busy serving Him. It is possible to serve Him and forget that we are serving Him. There is no other person

or situation that can ever take us away from the presence of the living God. He is ever with us, hearing our cries and helping and protecting us from danger, watching what we do. He is our ever-present God, Saviour, Lord, and Master – our dearest friend.

God Is Infinite

God has no limits or boundaries, and nothing can limit Him. He is not confined to dimensions, places, or space. His love, holiness, grace, mercy, and all His other qualities are unlimited in their scope and expression. He is full and rich. There is no end in God.

God Is Self-Existent

He has no beginning or end because He is the Creator. He is the only one who exists outside of the created order. God does not need our help or ideas to function. His foolishness is too much wisdom unto us (1 Corinthians 1: 25).

God Is Eternal

He is not bound by the dimension of time, and He is not in levels and capacities. He created time as a temporary context for His creation. With God, everything that has ever happened or will ever happen has already occurred within His awareness (it was predestined), and He encompasses all of eternity. He is the eternity, meaning He is past, present, and eternal.

God Is Self-Sufficient

Creation relies on God for existence or survival, as He has no need for anything. He does not need our help, and with all He does, He offers us the privilege of being involved with Him in the fulfilment of His purposes. God is gloriously incomprehensible, but He is also a personal spirit. Through His infinite love and goodness, He has provided a way for us to have an authentic, personal, and open relationship with Him. He does not feed from human hands, and He does not take anything from anyone. In fact, it's we who eat from His hands and need Him entirely in everything.

First, God revealed Himself to us in His word. The scriptures provide us with a clear description of what God is like, what is important to Him, and what He says who He is. We have split knowledge of who He is. Hebrews 1: 1 says that in the past, God revealed Himself in various ways. He didn't want to be concealed and remain unknown to us. At the same time, we can never come to know Him fully. He is bigger than we imagined.

Second, God came down from heaven to live on earth. John 1: 14 says that for thirty-three years, human beings could observe the incarnate son of the living God through their senses as they walked and talked with Jesus Christ.

Third, God destroyed the barrier of sin and self-centeredness that separated us from our holy God. The veil was taken away from us. Jesus died on the cross to pay the penalty for our sins and in the process gave us access to the Father.

Fourth, God sent the Holy Spirit to dwell in Christians with His presence.

Our Creator God did all this so we could go beyond just knowing about Him to actually be with Him. We can actually enter into His holiness and fellowship and have an intimate family relationship with Him.

God Is All-Powerful

Jeremiah 32: 17: God spoke the universe into being. It is a universe that astronomers estimate contains more than 100 billion galaxies. But all the power contained in the entire universe is but a small representation of the unlimited power that God possesses. The combined energy of all earth's storms, wind, ocean waves, and other forces of nature do not equal even a fraction of His absolute power. God's power is inherent in His nature; He gives it at will. All power has always been His and will continue to be His for all eternity. Any power that we have is given to us by God (John 1: 12). Because God is all-powerful, He has the ability to do whatever pleases Him. Again, His power is not restrained or inhibited by any of His creation. People and nations are powerless when confronted by God. He is capable of doing anything, and it does not even violate any of His attributes. No task is too big for Him, and He never fails or fails anyone. He is never tired, frustrated, or discouraged

Reflections/ Notes:

CHAPTER II

Use What You Have

Philippians 2: 9–10: As believers in Christ, we have been given the power of attorney to use the name of Jesus. If, for instance, someone comes to you with the request in the name of his boss, an authority figure you recognize, you will oblige him not because of who he is as a messenger but because of the respect you have for the one in whose name he has come. Even if you do not like the messenger's face or attitude, your respect for his boss will compel you to grant his request. The name of Jesus works the same way in the spirit realm.

John 16: 23: Peter understood this when he met the crippled man at the gate of the temple called Beautiful. That is why he said what he did to him in Acts 3: 6–7 ("Silver or gold have I none, but such as I have give I thee. In the name of Jesus Christ of Nazareth rise up and walk."). He took him by his right hand and lifted him up. Immediately, his crippled foot and ankle bones received strength. This was not a prayer. Peter did not make a request to God. He used the name of Jesus as an instrument.

When God sent Moses to Egypt to lead the Israelites out of bondage, He transformed his shepherd's rod supernaturally into an instrument of power. Exodus 4: 2–4 says, "And the Lord said unto him" What is that in your hand?" and he said "a rod" and He said cast it on the ground. And he cast it on the ground and it became a serpent and Moses fled from before it, and the Lord said take it by the tail, and he put forth his hand and caught it again by the tail." You have something far better than the rod, and that is the precious name of Jesus of Nazareth. When you make demands based on the instrumentality of the name of Jesus, the Lord will see to it that it is done. "If you shall ask anything in my name, I will do it" (John 14: 14).

A story of the widow who cried to Elijah as she had only a handful of meal in the barrel and a little oil to prepare for herself and her son so that they could eat and die as there was massive drought in the land (1 Kings 17: 12–16). This woman did not say that she had nothing. Because she disclosed the little she did have, she received her breakthrough and miracle. Until the rain came, she and her son had enough meal and oil.

Remember the story of another widow who cried to Elisha as her husband was dead, leaving her with huge debts and the creditors were coming to take her two sons to be slaves to pay back their father's debts? Elisha asked the woman what she had in her house, and she said that she had just a pot of oil. The woman received her miracle by telling the truth (2 Kings 4: 1–7).

Never say that you have nothing because the truth is that you do have something. You have the name of Jesus, a mighty and wonderful instrument to use. The disciples also understood this. When they told Jesus that the only food they had to feed a multitude was two fishes and five loaves of bread, Jesus blessed the food and gave it to the disciples to share with the multitude of people who all ate and were left full and contented. The disciples were aware that Jesus would multiply the food and feed the crowds, but to a carnal mind, there is no logic in this. Brethren, use the name of Jesus. It is a wonderful, powerful, and miraculous name. Ask anything in the name of Jesus, and you will get it. Our God is a good God who never tells lies like man; this is the heritage of being born again (Numbers 23: 19).

You and the Holy Spirit

The Holy Spirit

John 14: 26: Jesus promised His disciples and let them know that when He went back to the Father who had send Him before, He was not going to leave them alone. Rather, he would send the comforter. Jesus did not say He was going to teach us some new or strange things, but all things. The comforter the Holy Spirit was going to bring all the things that Jesus has taught to remembrance.

John 16: 7 and 16: 13–15: The disciples found it rather difficult to easily comprehend what Jesus was saying, why He was saying it, and why was He be leaving so soon. After a full study of the gospels, we can see how confused the disciples were at times when Jesus spoke to them.

Acts 1: 4 and 1: 8: The disciples stayed in Jerusalem and waited for the promise of the Father.

Acts 2: 1: Immediately after this happened, the disciples went about with power and miraculous signs and wonders. Being filled with the Holy Spirit also filled them with love. The early church did not have the Bible to read like we do. It had to rely on the Holy Spirit to teach and guide its followers. The Old Testament saints did not experience baptism in the Holy Spirit or indwelling. The Holy Spirit came upon them only for specific tasks as God needed and directed and would then leave. They did not have the Holy Spirit (power) in them to help them change. As a result, they kept rebelling against God's will. Do you not know that we have the Spirit of God dwelling in us? We have this treasure in earthly vessels. Some people say that we do not think that this Holy Ghost is for us, but in this next scripture, pay attention to what Jesus says.

Luke 11: 13: "If ye then, being evil, know how to give good gifts unto your children: how much more shall your heavenly Father give the Holy Spirit to them that ask him."

He was teaching here that all you have to do is ask and that you will receive the Holy Spirit. It is for everyone to believe and receive the gift of the Holy Spirit, but you have to do something. Ask. You need the Holy Spirit to understand the things of the spirit on which your natural mind cannot. Jesus taught Nicodemus that he must be born again to understand the kingdom of God because flesh cannot understand the things of the spirit. We are too human. Some time ago, before I was saved, I tried to study the Bible, and it did not make sense. If you have not been born again, it will not make sense to you. If you have been born again and the Holy Spirit lives in you, but if you do not believe, He will indwell quietly and not interfere. He is a perfect gentleman and will not force you to depend on him. Remember, Jesus said in John 14: 16–18: "Even the Spirit of truth; whom the world cannot receive, because it seeth him not, neither knoweth him: but ye know him; for he dwelleth with you, and shall be in you. I will not leave you comfortless: I will come to you."

In this life as children of God, we do need comfort, but sometimes, we think that we have no one around when we need that comfort. Look at what Jesus just said and did, though: He would not leave us comfortless. We do have and need the comforter all the times.

The Holy Spirit is real and living in us, longing to be a part of our lives and a close friend. He cannot wait to collaborate with us, and He wants to guide us in every area if we allow him and can involve Him in the decisions. Remember, He is the spirit of truth and of the living God. Even though a child of God lives in the world, we are not of this world, and we are to think on only the things from above. We can do that only with the Holy Spirit. Sometimes, the things around us will try to draw us away from God, but with the Holy Spirit guiding and teaching, we will not fall away or miss our way.

The Holy Spirit works in us. He is our partner, friend, and comforter. He teaches us to love those we do not want to love and those that have hurt us. He teaches us how to forgive those who do not deserve to be forgiven.

It is only through allowing Him to possess our lives that we do that.

1 John 2: 20: "But ye have an unction from the Holy One, and ye know all things."

1 John 2: 27: Let's see also what the Word of God says.

Romans 8: 26: "Likewise the Spirit also helpeth our infirmities: for we know not what we should pray for as we ought: but the Spirit itself maketh intercession for us with groanings which cannot be uttered. And he that searcheth the hearts knoweth what the mind of the Spirit is because he maketh intercession for the saints according to the will of God."

The Holy Spirit does not only intercede for us, but He does it in accordance with God's will. Romans 8 has so many promises about the Holy Spirit. I encourage you to read all of Romans 8. You will be blessed.

In my traditional background, I was not taught about having a personal relationship with Jesus, so I tried to do everything without the power of the Holy Spirit. It was failure after failure. I tried to change my life and was amazed that the changes were only temporary. At some point, I would try to forgive and forget, but it was so hard. I thought I knew how to love but realized that my efforts were not good enough. I did not understand peace or its effects, because I seldom had peace. Moreover, when I went through trials, I would panic and become restless. I would always look at the circumstances and could not see a way out and would not have an idea of how I would see any possibilities of safety. Then there was this other unforgettable, special day that something wonderful happened to my life. I met the Holy Ghost, and from that day, my life has not been the same. He has taught me what real nature of love and loving is, how to have joy, how to have peace even in the midst of a storm, and how to forgive and forget. He has revealed so much to me that I could not understand without Him. I find the mysteries of the hidden Word of God opened. Indeed, the word is full of hidden treasures that need the Holy Spirit to unfold.

Ephesians 4: 30: Do you know it grieves the Holy Spirit when we abandon Him and fail to involve Him in our daily life?

You have to know that the Holy Spirit is real.

The Holy Spirit Saved My Life

I want to give you an illustration of something in the natural. After you wash your hair, most people want to dry it with a hair dryer, which is good, but think upon this. You have to do something before you can get the dryer to work. You have to plug it in, so it can receive the power to serve its purpose. The Holy Spirit lives in you, but if you do not plug into Him, you cannot walk in the power of the anointing. All you need is to get him connected to you as he connects to the Father.

1 John 2: 27: Paul had an amazing revelation about the Holy Spirit, and he later knew that without the Holy Spirit, he was nothing. Through Him, though, he could do all things.

My Testimony

I was born and brought up in a Christian home and family. Going to church was part and parcel of daily life to me.

The church I attended did not emphasize the importance of being born again or baptism in the Holy Spirit. At that time, I was fine and comfortable with that because I did not know any other way. It took me a long time to arrive at my destination of truth. Eventually, I was born again, but I still did not have an insight into the Holy Spirit. I used to attend church as usual, sitting in the back, singing, praising, worshiping, giving my offering, and going home blessed. My friend, who was my pastor as well, told me about Joyce

Meyer coming to the town and visiting another church. We made plans to be there, not knowing it was to be my day of visitation by the Holy Spirit.

After a powerful, spirit-filled sermon, an altar call was made to those who wanted to accept the Lord Jesus as their personal Saviour. People came from all corners of the hall. Other calls were made for different needs, including healing. I was still seated, contented with the service and the miracles I had witnessed, seeing people getting healed. The last call was made for all those who wanted to be baptized in the Holy Ghost. I never thought twice, and I found myself in front with my hands raised high up, praising, praying, and worshipping like never before. Joyce laid her hands on me and anointed me. I cannot remember what happened after that, but I received the Holy Ghost from there up to now.

Now I cannot sit still in church without saying something to brethren. Everywhere I go, I talk about my Saviour, freely and boldly everywhere I go. The Holy Spirit gives you liberty as He is the spirit of Liberty (2 Corinthians 3: 17).

My friend was happy and surprised at the power of the Holy Spirit that was happening as she gazed on. It is no longer a big issue to stand in front and share my testimonies, give a word of exhortation, preach the word, or conduct any form of activity in church. I have learned He is a gift of God to all who believe (Luke 24: 49).

He is the spirit of love, power, and a sound mind. He makes a person an effective witness for Jesus. I can assure you that you will never remain the same once you have received the Holy Spirit. He will teach you how to live a holy life and how to glorify God (John 16: 13–14).

You can invite the Holy Spirit to come into your life, and He will. As you pray invite Him into your life, acknowledge His presence in your life. Talk to Him about all your daily encounters. He will solve them all for you. Allow the Holy Spirit full control of you and over your situation. Even if you encounter difficulties, knowing who is in you and by your side always gives you courage. I am talking from practical experience. I have been there and experienced Him, and I am practically involved with Him. You can also involve Him in all aspects of your daily encounters as you walk and fellowship with Him.

When you have the Holy Spirit in you, sitting still is practically impossible in church-related matters. You participate fully in the things of God. This particular Sunday service, it happened that I was the one preaching and the Holy Spirit gave me this subject to preach on: Who is the Holy Spirit to a Christian and what is the Holy Spirit's job description?

The Holy Spirit will teach you the truths and guide you into all truths. He will teach you all things concerning God and His kingdom. You cannot live a successful Christian life without the Holy Spirit. He is your helper in understanding the Word of God and all mysteries and makes life liveable or easier for you (2 Kings 2: 8–9).

As it came to pass when they had crossed over the Jordan that Elijah said to Elisha, "ask what I shall do for you."

Elisha said, "I pray thee let a double portion of thy spirit upon me." After finishing explaining the part of scripture, I had an altar call for those who wanted to be laid hands on and also that they would receive the gift of the Holy Spirit. I also extended the call to those who were interested in receiving of a double portion of the same Spirit. Most brethren came forward. We had no anointing oil at hand, but we used what we had: the name of Jesus, passing the anointing unto them. Within a few seconds, people fell under the anointing. We continued to praise the power of the living God through the Holy Spirit, singing hymns and songs of praise and rejoicing in the Lord. I then spoke to one lady who also received the free gift of the Holy Ghost. She gave her testimony that she had received the Holy Spirit. She said that she felt a gush of hot current like lightning powerfully striking her down. She got up, and she was full of the anointing. I gave glory to God for He reigns and for performing such a wonderful touch on His people

and using us as His vessels. I witnessed this as did the whole congregation. Praise be to God forever and ever. Amen.

Walking In the Spirit

If we are to walk in the spirit, we then must become faithful and diligent enough to spend the time it takes to get to know God intimately. It will be difficult to trust in Him if you do not get to know Him personally. We have this personal relationship with the Father through our Lord Jesus and have solid foundation in the Word. By walking in that spirit realm, we can absolutely dominate the things on this earth.

Galatians 5: 16: "This I say then, Walk in the Spirit, and ye shall not fulfil the lust of the flesh."

Galatians 5: 25: "if we live in the Spirit, let us also walk in the Spirit."

You should then strive to be able to walk in the Spirit even though you are in the flesh. We have to spend more time pursuing the things of the Spirit rather than the flesh (carnal). We are well able to do this by dedicating ourselves to the Word of God and be willing to take the time from daily pursuits. Moreover, our natural abilities or talents cannot determine our usefulness. All we have to do is live in His presence and seek His guidance and help over our personal abilities. We naturally look and are eager to find who has this ability here and there, but only God does not look for ability. Rather, He looks for availability. Therefore, you can make yourself available to God and the Holy Spirit by praying in the spirit, worshipping, and fellowshipping with Him. Soon, there will be a full manifestation of His character, nature, glory, and spirit in you. Jesus is not on earth anymore, so God reproduced Jesus's character in us, the believers, so the world can know Him through those who have been saved.

Overcoming

This is the overwhelming battle that happens daily in every Christian life. Have you noticed that you are sometimes aware of certain things before you even know what the Word of God say regarding them? This is so because the Holy Spirit is always ahead of us. He gives us insight of what is and what is to come. We shall, however, see this in the following topics (John 16: 13).

Spiritual Failure is Due to the Weakness of the Flesh

Mat 26: 40–41 and Acts 2: 26: We have allowed our flesh to dominate us because of a lack of knowledge of the living Word of God.

Galatians 5: 25–26: "If we live in the Spirit, let us also walk in the Spirit. Let us not be desirous of vain glory, provoking one another, envying one another."

Your flesh or body is like a puppy. It will do whatever you train it to do. However, if you give attention to the things of the world, your flesh has a natural hunger for the things of the world. Your danger is also in yoking yourself to canal people with canal ideas and missions. Remember he who is willing to sin with you will also sin against you. Envy, strife, rage, and jealously are also sins that will shut the door to the blessings of God and will likewise open the door to the Devil. Unforgiveness will make you ill and is the fountain of depression, heart disease, memory loss, and other ailments. Be careful not to expose yourself to the things of the world. Your body will dominate you into these cravings.

Practicing the things of the spirit will cause you to overcome the desires of the flesh. Your spirit should dominate your flesh if you continue meditating the word and confessing the word (homologio) until your heart ignites to praying (without ceasing).

1 Thessalonians 5: 17: "Pray without ceasing."

Matthew 26: 41: "Watch and pray, that ye enter not into temptation: the spirit indeed is willing, but the flesh is weak."

Be more of a doer of the Word and not merely a hearer and keep reminding the Holy Spirit that you do rely on Him. To experience a more effective experience, ask the Holy Spirit to show you things in yourself that need changing. Trust His help, and He will help you through. You will soon walk into a new level of your spiritual growth when you start applying these principles.

Speaking in Other Tongues

Many charismatic people – Christians included – fail to understand the true benefits of speaking in other tongues, nor why this gift is so valuable to the body of Christ. Here are a couple reasons why we need this gift.

Ø From the beginning, the manifestation that came with the gift of the Holy Spirit was speaking in other tongues. It was not the wind, trance, fire, noise, or feeling of God's presence that was evidence of the gift being received, but spirit-filled believers as he began to speak the languages of the spirit. They did not understand themselves. Neither did the onlookers. It was God's plan for the gift to function as a spiritual language (Acts 2: 4). 1 Corinthians 14: 2 says, "For he that speaketh in an unknown tongue speaketh not unto men, but unto God: for no man understandeth him; howbeit in the spirit he speaketh mysteries."

Ø Jesus commanded, prayed, and taught us to receive the gift of the Holy Spirit. After the commissioning of the disciples to wait in Jerusalem until they received the promise of the Father, Jesus did not say, "Do this if you feel led to do so or if it fits in your doctrinal or denominational beliefs, or if you have the time to, or if you are so inclined, or if you feel comfortable about it." He instructed them to tarry until they received the gift of the Holy Spirit. The Lord Jesus put such importance on their receiving the Holy Spirit. That is more than enough reason for every Christian to seek God until they receive the gift (Acts 1: 4 and 5: 32, John 14: 16 – 17, and Ephesians 5: 18).

The Word of God exhorts us to be filled with the spirit and to pray in the new tongues. The spirit language enables us to live in the spirit, walk in the spirit, be led of the spirit, have the fruit of the Spirit, manifest the gifts of the spirit, and go from glory to glory until we are transformed to His full image (Galatians 5: 22–25, Romans 8: 14, 1 Corinthians 12: 7–11, and Ephesians 5: 18).

1 Corinthians 14: 15: "what is it then? I will pray with the spirit, and I will pray with the understanding also: I will sing with the spirit, and I will sing with the understanding also."

Acts 19: 2: "He said unto them: Have ye received the Holy Ghost since ye believed? And they said unto him: We have not so much as heard whether there be any Holy Ghost."

Ø Speaking in tongues is the greatest gift the Holy Spirit ever gave to a believer. Jesus is the greatest gift God could give for the redemption of the world, and the Holy Spirit is the greatest gift Jesus could give to His bride the church. 1 Corinthians 14: 4 says, "He that speaketh in an unknown tongue edifieth himself; but he that prophesieth edifieth the church."

Ø Speaking in tongues enables us to have spirit-to-Spirit communication with God. Humans are spirit beings living in the flesh-and-bone bodies. While man's sin deadened the spirit, Jesus brings the spirit back to life by imparting His everlasting life into us. The Holy Spirit gives us a spirit language so we can communicate directly with God (John 4: 24 and 3: 3–5,16).

Ø Praying in tongues also builds and increases our faith (1 Corinthians 15: 45). Faith is the medium of exchange for all heavenly things, just as money is the medium of exchange for all earthly things. It is at this trading point that a lot of good things are changed, sorrow for joy, poverty for riches, and so on. A major way to increase our faith is to always pray in tongues. "But ye, beloved, building up yourselves on your most holy faith, praying in the Holy Ghost" (Jude 1: 20).

Ø Praying in tongues activates the fruit of the Spirit. It is beneficial to have each of the spiritual attributes become active and mature in us. The fruits of the spirit or gift do not grow in us, but we do grow in them. Praying in tongues helps us fulfil God's predestined purpose for us to be conformed to the image Christ Jesus (Galatians 5: 22–23, 1 Corinthians 13: 1–13, and 2 Corinthians 3: 18).

Ø Praying in spirit is the main way we fulfil the scriptural admonition to pray without ceasing. Believers can pray in tongues at any time. If we are in a place where it is not convenient or wise to speak out loud in tongues, we can pray with our inner man without making an audible sound (Ephesians 6: 18).

Matthew 26: 41 says, Watch and pray, that ye enter not into temptation: the spirit indeed is willing, but the flesh is weak."

In Luke 18: 1 and 21: 36 as well as 1 Corinthians 14: 15, the Holy Spirit directs this language and tells us to pray in accordance with the will of God. Probably the only time we can be assured that we are praying in the will of God is when we are praying in spirit. God always answers requests that are made in alignment with His will (Romans 8: 27 and 1 John 5: 14–15).

My family and friends and I went for a long weekend holiday in Aberystwyth, Mid Wales. It was an enjoyable experience, travelling with my family and relatives. The weekend went well, and we thanked God as a norm and asked the Almighty for journey mercies when coming back to England. As usual, we had a first break at the filling station and then left again. I was in the third lane of motorway when my daughter said that she could hear funny noises coming from the car I was driving. As I also listened carefully and checked on exactly where the noises were coming from, we all agreed that it was on the driver's side. The motorway was busy at that time, and most people were coming from work and holidays as we were too.

I was not going to stop there, and without wasting time,

I started to pray in other tongues and spoke to the Holy Ghost out loud. I never mumbled or doubted to whom I was speaking. This went on for fifteen minutes without ceasing. Let me remind you that I was still on the motorway on the third lane and driving at top speed with no thought of slowing down. When I said amen, all the funny noises suddenly disappeared. We were amazed at what had happened. I then went back to praying in tongues, acknowledging the presence of the Holy Spirit in our midst and thanking Him for the good work He had done in preventing what could have been a disaster to our lives. This prayer went on again for another fifteen minutes without ceasing. When we arrived at the next filling station, my daughters started telling other family members and friends what has happened in our car. We all gathered there and worshipped Him, and we praised and gave Him all the adoration and glory. We continued with our journey until we arrived home safe, healthy, and full of joy. Even today, we are still rejoicing in the name of Jesus.

Another Sunday, I was in church when two police officers came in and asked the ushers for a sister. This sister went in a private room with these officers. When she came out after a lengthy time, she wanted to share what was going on with the church. She explained that it was a Wednesday evening when she was coming from a midweek church service as she walked alone by the main road that was fully lit up. There was a car that pulled up, and four men kidnapped her. She screamed and kicked, but there was no one to rescue her. Two of the four men sat with her at the back seat. She thought that she going to die or that they would assault or rape her, but in the midst of all the confusion, she said she remembered the pastor preaching to not be afraid or intimidated. God has not given you the spirit of fear but of power love and a sound mind. You have a sound mind, and you are full of power to operate in your anointing and speaking in the Holy Ghost.

As she sat there and started to quietly speak in tongues, the car was moving at a high speed. She could not see where it was heading. The sister began to increase the tone of her voice as she spoke in other tongues. The men became restless, agitated, and irritated by this and told her to keep quiet or they would assault her. They shouted at her as she shouted her prayers. They argued among themselves. The man at the back shouted at the driver to turn the heater off, and the driver answered it was not on, but they felt a terrible heat wave that that made it unbearable to be in the car. The sister never stopped praying in the spirit. They were sweating, but it was winter. The driver decided to stop the car in the middle of the road, leaving the engine running, and they left running for their lives but there was nobody chasing them. The sister said she got out of the car still in the spirit mode, thanking and praising the Almighty God for His presence that filled the car. The thieves who came to kill steal and destroy left without doing any of that. The sister was left free, unharmed, alive, and rejoicing in the name of Jesus. Praise the Lord! Halleluiah!

The Gifts of the Spirit

Spiritual Gifts (1 Corinthians 12: 1–11)

In the life of the local church, there are two major problems equating to the subject regarding spiritual gifts. The first few Christians were conceived of themselves as spectators rather than participants. We shall assume that on the basis of our study of Ephesians 4: 16, you would no longer consider this a viable option, along with those who are actively involved in the ministry of the local church but who are not functioning in a ministry that corresponds to their spiritual gifts. The solution to both these problems is a proper understanding of the subject of spiritual gifts. It is my contention that Bible expositors have often made of this subject something far more mystical and mysterious and complicated than it really is. You know that if there is anyone who can look at a matter with simplicity, it is me.

Know Your Spiritual Gift

There are several reasons many have played down the importance of knowing your spiritual gift. We will begin our study of spiritual gifts by suggesting several reasons why it is imperative for every Christian to know his or her area of gifting.

- The prominence of spiritual gifts in scripture. The simplest way we can measure the paramount importance of a principle or a doctrine is to determine

The amount of space devoted to it in the Word of God. Subjects or doctrines that are merely implied are surely of less significance than those clearly stated or repeated. Matters mentioned infrequently should not be regarded as crucial as those frequently dealt with. Using this standard of measurement to the subject of spiritual gifts is a vital as we find gifts addressed specifically in four major scriptures: 1 Corinthians 12–14; Romans 12; Ephesians 4; and 1 Peter 4. In addition to these central passages, spiritual gifts are mentioned elsewhere in the Bible. Spiritual gifts must be important to the spirit of God who inspired the writing of the Word of God.

- The embryonic nature of spiritual gifts. After the first epistle to the church at Corinth was written, it was addressed to those who were obviously not very mature in their faith. There were many forms of carnality cited by Paul in this epistle. The things of which Paul wrote in this letter were not matters of the deeper life, but rather the elemental truths of the Christian life. Due to the emphasis on spiritual gifts in 1 Corinthians, we conclude that the doctrine of spiritual gifts is crucial.

Spiritual gifts are a matter of individual stewardship. Peter spoke of spiritual gifts as a matter of personal stewardship (1 Peter 4: 10). He meant that just as we must give account of our use of the material things God has placed under our control, we must also be accountable for the use of our spiritual gifts.

It is unwise or rather difficult to be a good steward of something we do not know about and of something that we do not even know we have in our possession.

Spiritual gifts are of great practical value and benefit to believers. We want to assume few areas of practical benefit.

a. **Knowing your spiritual gift will enable you to find your place of ministry in the body of Christ.** Since every Christian has a particular function in the body of Christ, and since your spiritual gifts equip you to carry out this function, knowing your gift helps.

b. **Knowing your spiritual gift will enable you to determine your priorities.** One of the most common problems we all face is having more things to do than we have time for. You must know your spiritual gifts to set these priorities (Romans 12: 6–8).

c. **Knowing your spiritual gift will help in discerning God's will.** The choice of your occupation, whether secular or religious, should take into account whether it will help or hinder the exercise and development of your spiritual gift (as well as the nature of people around you). If you are not gifted to teach, you have a valuable insight into

God's will when you are offered a teaching position. There is a very distinct relationship between knowing the will of God and understanding your spiritual gift.

Purposes of Spiritual Gifts

A simple definition of a spiritual gift would be the Godgiven capacity of every Christian to carry out his function in the body of Christ.

The thrust of the first half of Ephesians 4 is that the effective functioning of the body of Christ is dependent upon the contribution of each individual who is part of the body of Christ. Spiritual gifts enable us to carry out our task within the body of Christ in a way that no one else can in their natural state. In using the analogy of the physical body in 1 Corinthians 12, there is the reinforcement of this same concept. Every part of the body is essential to the well-being of the total body. When one member fails to do his part, the whole body is in trouble.

There are two important corollaries to this truth that spiritual gifts equip the Christian to carry out his unique contribution to the body.

1. Spiritual gifts are not primarily given to benefit certain groups or an individual but the entire body of Christ. Anyone who seeks a spiritual gift and employs it to give himself a kind of spiritual high is

missing the point and purpose of the spiritual gift. Perhaps this is the most serious criticism of the contemporary tongues movement. The Lord Jesus did not raise a single gift above all the others. The primary purpose of this gift seems to be self-edifying in one body.

2. If spiritual gifts are given to enable us to carry out every essential function of the body, we should expect spiritual gifts that correspond to every function described in the scriptures.

Just as we see that all are to engage in the exercise of these functions, there are gifts that overlap these functions. These are those who are gifted in these various capacities and will excel in a certain function.

Common Misconceptions of Spiritual Gifts

Before we go on to the subject of discovering your gift, I want to take a moment to deal with some of the most common errors we make or hear regarding gifts of the spirit.

Element 1: Confusing Spiritual Gifts with Spirituality

The great error of the carnal Corinthian church was that they confused spiritual gifts with spirituality. Those who spoke in tongues thought themselves to be notches higher on the spiritual plateau than those who had not received the gift. The Corinthian church was apparently an exceptionally gifted church, but it was also one of the most carnal churches ever mentioned in the New Testament. The one with the gift of giving may be far more spiritual than the evangelist who is winning thousands to Christ. Let us recall the Old Testament figure Samson and be reminded that while he was performing great feats of strength, he was living a life devoted to the flesh. It took Delilah, who had no inch of muscle, to do the unthinkable.

Element 2: Our Spiritual Gift Excuses Us from Other Responsibilities

The watchword of the Christian sluggard is "That is not my gift." My pet peeve is the pastor-teacher who maintains that his sole obligation is to prepare for sermons. He has no time for counselling those who are struggling with life and cannot visit the sick or comfort the mourning. In this same attitude and mind is an abuse of the biblical teaching concerning spiritual gifts. We have demonstrated that every gift relates to a function that is the responsibility of every believer. While our gifts necessitate that we establish priorities, we are never excused from the responsibilities.

Element 3: Obsession for Knowledge about Spiritual Gifts

We now have already stressed the importance of knowing our spiritual gifts. Let us now make it clear that knowledge is not so important that we neglect service thereof. There is in my estimation far too much intellectualism in some Christian circles or communities.

Paul had to say to the Corinthians, "Knowledge puffs up, but love builds up" (1 Corinthians 8: 1). Many Christians insist upon knowing what their spiritual gifts are before they begin to serve God in any capacity. One can tell that they are more interested in studying and knowing than in serving to their own advantage. It is my contention that we learn our spiritual gifts as we serve and as we devote ourselves to the service of others. We will inevitably learn what our gifts are. I am not negating the importance of study or doctrine. Simply, our motive should be to learn to serve, not to study simply to learn.

Element 4: Defining Spiritual Gifts in Terms of the Spectacular

We have made two serious mistakes. One is that we have focused upon extraordinary gifts, and most of us are not going to get close to their level of effectiveness. In addition to confusing the effectiveness of different individuals with the same spiritual gift, we also ignore the different spheres of ministry that God has for the same gift. We erroneously suppose that evangelism must take place in a coliseum rather than around a coffee table. We think teaching must be done behind a pulpit rather than on the back porch. It is no wonder that many Charismatics seriously question whether they possess some spiritual gift. It is often because they are trying to measure their gifts against the giants.

How Can I Discover My Spiritual Gift

Let us now consider how one can learn what his or her spiritual gift is in the body of Christ. With this hope, you have concluded that this matter is not the great mystery we have made it out to be. God has given you a gift, and He intends for you to know your gift and you develop in it and eventually use it for His glory in ministry. Gifts are not classified or top-secret material intended for only the spiritual elite. However, we have to arrive at a simple and concise definition for each of the spiritual gifts recorded in the scriptures. We must also note that there are gifts we see in the New Testament that are not operational in the Old Testament. These are vocal gifts of the spirit.

The gift of faith is the supernatural ability to trust God. Faith is both active and passive. The housewife, for example, may demonstrate active faith by trusting God to establish a Bible study for ladies in the neighbourhood. The husband may exercise active faith in stepping out into a new type of business venture that will bring additional opportunities for ministry. Passive faith is faith that hangs on for dear life. The seminary wife with the gift of faith may demonstrate her passive faith when all the obstacles point to her husband throwing in the towel and quitting seminary, but she keeps encouraging him to trust. These kinds of faith benefit the body by encouraging others to trust the Lord both actively and passively.

Whatever you do, do not define the gifts in terms of the spectacular. Instead, define the gifts as they relate to you and the situation at hand. For example, consider how the gift of faith would manifest itself in your situation, on the job, at home, and in your given responsibilities at your local church. Most of the gifts are dormant because they have not been exercised, and in some cases, the one who has the gift fails to submit to authority. Most importantly, obey the scriptures and submit to the man and woman of God so you can learn more and grow. Most Christians do not know what their spiritual gifts are. The point is that they have never tried to find out.

If I am to ask you what are your natural abilities are, the first thing that you would do is to ask yourself whether you have tried to search within yourself. The general imperatives of the scriptures have made it easy for us. The Word of God commands us to do everything that corresponds to some spiritual gift.

Obeying the scriptures will direct us in doing the things that you see need to be done easily and more efficiently, and nothing can be done to quiet that Bible-natured gift. There is virtually no way you can keep a gifted teacher quiet. There is always the sense and a need to teach if given the chance. He meets that need by sharing what he knows to be God, God's ways and the greater mysteries yet to be unveiled, and giving of answers to questions at hand. Those gifted in the area of giving are the ones who are most sensitive to financial needs. They do have a sense in them that goes over everyone else's heads. With every spiritual gift comes the ability to discern the need as well as the ability to meet needs within all spiritual outfits.

I do, however, suggest that individuals react to given situations in light of their gifts. These reactions are never the same in two people. For example, the gift of administration delegates, organizes issues, works to avoid confusion, and gives direction. At the same time, teaching suggests some ways to avoid a recurrence of the problem. However, children of God let us learn to devote ourselves to what we do best. As we have seen earlier (that you do not do some things very well is no indication that you are to cease altogether in that area), this should be a tip as to where you should concentrate efforts. On the basis of your own evaluation and the suggestions of those you respect, begin to devote more time and energy to what makes your gift grow and work more efficiently. If you are a teacher, spend time teaching. Gather materials that give you knowledge on teaching and meet and spend time with other teachers. This leads to the development of the gifts. Make the most of whatever opportunities come that will aid you in enhancing your spiritual gifts. Do not waste time and chances. Also, it is true that even a job change will help you develop your gift. If your gift is teaching, you may well consider a teaching occupation that will enhance your abilities in teaching. If you are particularly skilled in counselling, you may be able to find a job that gives you additional opportunities to develop these abilities.

Having been learning about spiritual gifts, there are no mysteries. You can know your gift; indeed, you must know your gift, be groomed in your gift, and grow in it. As you grow, you must recognize the great variety and diversity and not only inter gifts. There is diversity not only in the kinds of gifts but also in the areas of ministry of your gift and in the degree of success you will have with your gift. Do not make the mistake of measuring yourself against other spiritual gifted man and woman, and do not confuse spirituality with the greatness of your gift.

The biggest danger with gifted people is that they will let their gift go to their head or failure to use their gifts, thinking they will never be missed (Matthew 25: 24–30).

The success of the body of Christ is proportional to the effective working of each and every member (Ephesians 4: 16).

However, it could then be possible that you are considering spiritual gifts, when in reality, you have never come to receive the gift of salvation through faith in the person and work of Jesus Christ on the cross. We should have an open mind to the fact that all of God's gifts are gifts of grace. The Holy Spirit gives them in spite of us rather than because of us. The fact remains that one will not receive spiritual gifts until you have first received the gift of salvation (be saved).

You must accept the verdict of God that you are a sinner and that you are living in rebellion against God's will and deserving of eternal punishment. Brothers and sisters, hell is real, and heaven is real. Make a good decision, and come to the point where you recognize that nothing you can ever do will ever merit God's eternal salvation. God so loved the world (you and me), and He gave us His Son Jesus to die in our place.

"For God so loved the world, that he gave his only begotten Son, that whosoever believeth in him should not perish, but have everlasting life" (John 3: 16).

The gift of salvation is made possible through the sinless life and sacrificial death of Jesus Christ in the sinner's place: your place and my place, thus for the poor, rich, educated, wise – everyone. If you trust in Him as the one who died for you, who took your punishment and exchanged your sin for His righteousness, you too can receive the gift of salvation. When you have done this, you will also discover that God has also given you the gift of His Spirit and the spiritual ability to contribute to the ongoing work of His body, the church. Make a choice that will have an everlasting impact on your life eternally. Are you so sure that if Jesus were to return today to take the saints, are you in a position to say you would go with Him? If you were to die today, do you know where you will go? Do you know that this earth and its glory will shade and fade away? It is true, but why do you not change your final destination to be with God and have eternal life through Jesus by praying a simple prayer? After praying, find a Bible-teaching church. I want to pray with you today and believe in your heart that Jesus died for your sins. He is able to save you. Let's pray:

Dear God in heaven,

I come to you in this day and in the name of your son, Jesus. I acknowledge to you that I am a sinner and sinful have I been, and I am sorry for all my sins and the life that I have lived in disobedience to your holy word and will. I am sorry, God. I need your forgiveness.

I believe that Jesus Christ shed His precious blood on the cross at Calvary and died for my sins, and I am now willing to turn from my sin. I do refuse and reject the powers of darkness, and I turn away from the works of the Devil.

You said in your word (Romans 10: 9) that if I confess the Lord our God and believe in my heart that God raised Jesus from the dead, I shall be saved. Save me now, Lord.

Right now, I confess Jesus as the Lord of my soul, and with my heart today, yes, I do believe that God raised Jesus from the dead. Father God, this moment, hear me as I accept Jesus Christ as my own personal Saviour. Right now, I am saved.

Thank you, Lord Jesus, for your undeserved grace which has saved me from my sins this day in the name of Jesus. Come into my heart, Lord, save me, and write my name in the book of life, I pray. I believe that you have saved me. Thank you, Jesus, for dying for me and giving me eternal life. I receive you and your blood in my life, I pray.

Amen.

Testimony

During the compiling of this book series, I was working with my daughter Thembeka, who was helping me putting things in place for publishing. One of her friends was in trouble with family challenges and was at the verge of giving up on life as a suicidal spirit settled in. That time, there was no hope of trying again and written was a piece of a paper with a message of why the suicide would be committed. My daughter happened to know what her friend was going to do, and she called the friend up for a cup of coffee and a friendly talk. At that time, she was doing a few edits on this book when her friend arrived. She then started talking about this book and its contents. Soon, the spirit of God arrested the suicidal friend. As they kept reading, the spirit of suicide began to leave my daughter's friend. There was an immediate deliverance, and life was restored as the Holy Spirit took over the friend's life. Today, we are celebrating what the Lord has been doing changing lives. If you read this book prayerfully, it will mould you and change your life for better. Praise the Lord who is changing lives through this book.

As we shall see even more in the second volume of this book, I shall endeavour to answer or explain some subject topics and tips on:

- Can someone give you a clue of what your spiritual gift is?
- What do you do with this gift in your church?
- Does it mean that some gifts are more important than others?
- How do these gifts operate fully, and what are they?

We all have been given gifts of the spirit by the indwelling of the spirit of God.

Acts 2: 38: "Then Peter said unto them, Repent, and be baptized every one of you in the name of Jesus Christ for the remission of sins, and ye shall receive the gift of the Holy Ghost."

In Acts 8 and 1 Corinthians chapters 12–14, we see external gifts of the Holy Spirit.

The gifts have been developed by no human capacities. Rather, they were given for human use. Therefore, no one should not have glory in them. If we exalt in our God-given gifts, we take credit for the things that we have not earned ourselves. Moreover, it was a gift that was not yours in the first place but was then given to you freely, and it is given apart from your works or any inherent capabilities.

The spiritual gifts are there to empower and make the body of Christ complete. The gifts also are intended for the church to edify itself and to feed it, exhort it, and encourage it.

The gifts are important, and some of them are more similar in our perception but different from the nine gifts of the spirit mentioned in in 1 Corinthians 12:

1) Word of wisdom
2) Word of knowledge
3) Faith
4) Gifts of healing
5) Working of miracles

6) Prophecy
7) Discerning of spirits
8) Diverse kinds of tongues
9) Interpretation of other tongues

The Holy Spirit gives these spiritual gifts as He wills and not for what we think they are (verse 11). You cannot receive a particular spiritual gift that you do not intend to receive, but you can desire certain gifts, indicating that you can receive according the desire of your heart (verse 31). Contained in Romans 12 is a similar list of the gifts of the spirit. However, 1 Corinthians 12 is more comprehensive in narration on these gifts, and it begins with Paul telling the church at Corinth. Paul wanted to make these gifts clear to us so that we can deepen in understanding and depend upon the inspired Word of God to reveal them to us (verse 1). He teaches us that "There are different kinds of gifts, but the same Spirit distributes them" (verse 4).

No two gifts are the same, and no two believers have exactly the same gifts, but these gifts are always given for the common good of the church (verse 7).

"The fear of the LORD is the beginning of wisdom" (Proverbs 9: 10).

If a man follows the teaching of the Lord, he will gain good understanding. We are taught from the scriptures that the boy Solomon asked the Lord for wisdom. The Lord gave Solomon wisdom as well as wealth (1 Kings 3: 12). In wisdom, Solomon was able to understand what to do in difficult decisions. He was able to discern the language of animals and flowers as well as to understand things under the water. When the queen of Sheba visited Solomon, he made a water trough and placed mirrors at the bottom where the queen would pass through. As the queen passed through, stepping on the mirrors that were under the water, he would observe her feet. He picked a message left by her steps on top of the glass that was hidden in water. He was wise and very understanding of the emotions of men (without using words). His wisdom was divine. No one had ever come to half of what Solomon had in wisdom and wealth.

The fear of God is simply standing in awe of God in reverence and respect and entails loving God's Word and being obedient.

Gift of Knowledge

In principle, people have flap knowledge of God as well as His ways and works. It is not possible to fully understand the depth and knowledge of this God. As humans, we will come to a point where we end. However, the question is how to we know God. And can we handle His knowledge? In the Word of God, we are told that the children of Israel only knew and saw God's ways, acts, and signs that assumed His presence on the mountain. We know God through oral testimonies, and we know God by revelation and personal encounter. The term *Word of knowledge* is the utterance of knowledge. This is not God's knowledge, but it is knowledge of God's Word and ways. The Word here is certainly the Word of God. The utterance of knowledge could indicate that those with the gift of knowledge know when to speak the words and how to deliver the word.

Gift of Faith

In verse 9, the gifted people in this area tend to exude confidence in all situations but display a unique ability when operating in the gift. This is not the same as the saving faith that comes by hearing the word in Romans 10: 17. The gift speaks about that which God would provide while there is nothing to show for it, even though we know that God would always provide according to His ability and grace. Faith is a deep subject that needs a lot of care. There several kinds of faith that, when applied, could mean something very different in principle. The gifted person is more like godly, and he sees things that are not evident as if they already are. Find more regarding faith in the second volume of this book.

Gift of Healing

Healing has become a controversial subject. We are observing a host of ideologies and diverse methods and definitions on the subject of healing itself. This gift had been misunderstood. Some faith healers claim to have this gift, but have often been exposed to be frauds. The simplest thing any sufferer needs to know is that the name of Jesus alone heals. It does not need other supporting elements, but the name alone is enough to heal any manner of pain of disease. The subject needs to be approached with care, and the same principles on faith can still apply, although there is a huge difference between the two. The similarity is both gifts are given by the same spirit of the living God. Here, there is the idea of healing through faith. This gift was more prominent and is still. In the New Testament church, it confirms Jesus's name. I am not saying that people are still not healed today. There is a much higher healing wave that is sweeping across the continents, all in the name of our Lord, and Jesus is still healing many. The gift of healing is connected to the prayer of faith, and we know that the effectual prayer of a righteous man or woman can accomplish miracles (James 5: 16).

Gift of Miracles

This is also considered to be closely likened to the gift of faith. Miracles are jointly linked to faith. Jesus did not tell us that we should look for miracles. Rather, He said miracles shall follow us (Mark 16: 17). There is a difference between just miracles and the miracles performed because we do have a miracle worker who is operating under the gift. Any gift or its results are always credited to the Holy Spirit and never to humans. Miracles still occur today. Please note that there is the difference between miracles, signs, and wonders. The differences are explained further in the second volume of this book.

Gift of Prophecy (Speaking)

In verse 10, prophecies have several different interpretations. There is a lot to be learned about this gift as it is clear that in this context, in the church at Corinth, prophecy included teaching and/or speaking. To be a seasoned prophet takes a lot of time. We now understand that one is given the gift that will take a great deal in feeding with the right doctrine and much of hearing and listening to God for direction. The meaning here is that it is "publicly speaking" or "speaking forth" or "uttering forth" the Word of God.

Gift of Discernment

This was the cry of the Paul in all that he was writing to the churches. It is vital that we all work in this gift. The gift is about "distinguishing between spirits." It is a Godgiven ability to discern scriptures and their application and thereby the good and the wrong, earnest, and sincere. We see Peter operating in the gift in Acts 5 when Ananias and his wife, Sapphira, sold a piece of property, kept back part of the money, brought the rest, put it at the apostles' feet, but lied (Acts 5: 1–10). There are no errors when we move under this gift. It is vital because it eliminates wrong spirit from the right. Spiritual life is better under this gift, and all we can do is to yearn for the gift and ask and pray to the Lord.

Gift of Tongues

This is one of the missing vocal gifts in the old covenant. We do not see or hear about it in the Old Testament until David mentions the speaking of tongues in Psalms (verse 10). This is the most misunderstood gift. There is yet a difference between just speaking in tongues and having the gift of speaking in tongues. On the outpouring of the Holy Spirit on the day of Pentecost, many where given the ability to speak in tongues. Paul wrote and taught about tongues in 1 Corinthians 12–14 and in the process was reproving the Corinthians that this has been missing and that there was the misuse of the gift within the church. It is not as easy getting any kind of mandate to speak in tongues as what is given here contextually. It was a corrective order given to the church at Corinth. Every member in the body of Christ is a good candidate to this gifting.

Interpretation of Tongues

The gift of tongues is then associated with the gift of interpretation of tongues (verse 10). Since he who speaks in tongues speaks in an unknown language, there is the need for interpretation. This gift demands order, selfdiscipline, and control. 1 Corinthians 14: 33 notes that the interpretation is no carnal or human ability. Rather, it is a gifting by the same Holy Spirit. I can speak IsiZulu, Afrikaans, isiXhosa, IsiSotho, and English, but I cannot say that I have the gift of understanding the tongues I speak unless the Holy Spirit gives me that ability to translate them.

It is not the interpretation that you have to have to get yourself into school and learn a language unless the Holy Ghost empowers you. If you happen to find this is easy, then you may be imbued with such a gift. If anyone was speaking in tongues in the church, there should be someone absolutely there to interpret or they should remain silent. Paul continues to teach and say there should be not more than one person to speak in tongues because there is only one interpreter available to translate at one given moment. If there are several people speaking in tongues at the same time, this will bring confusion as God is not the author of confusion.

Other Gifts of the Spirit

Romans 12: 7–8 talks about additional gifts: "if it is serving, then serve; if it is teaching, then teach; if it is to encourage, then give encouragement; if it is giving, then give generously; if it is to lead, do it diligently; if it is to show mercy, do it cheerfully."

Many Gifts, Many Members, One Body

Everyone who is part and member of the church is clearly a part of the body of Christ, and we have diverse gifts and callings for the benefit of the same body. In the church, God has placed first apostles, prophets, teachers, and pastors (1 Corinthians 12: 28–31). My prayer for the body of Christ today is that we will not only seek and discover gifts but also that as a body with many members, we utilize them to the strengthening of the body of Christ.

Reflections/ Notes:

CHAPTER III

Jesus Christ

Chronology

We believe that Jesus was a true Galilean Jew. He was born at the beginning of the first century and was crucified and died between 30 and 36 AD in Judea. Jesus was a contemporary of John the Baptist (the forerunner) and was crucified by Roman governor Pontius Pilate, who held office from 26 to 36 AD. Both men died during Pilate's rule. Jesus lived in Galilee and Judea and did not preach or study anywhere else.

In Matthew 2: 1, it associates the birth of our Lord Jesus Christ with the reign of Herod, who died around 4 BC. Luke 1: 5 tells us that Herod reigned as king before the birth of Jesus. We should take care in noting that there was not only one Herod. Several emerged concurrently in accordance to their succession. However, we are told that the birth was during or towards the Census of Quirinius. John's ministry preceded Acts 10: 37–38 and was recorded in Luke 3: 1–2. It begun in the fifteenth year of Tiberius' reign. Dionysius was the first to use the Christian calendar era Anno Domini (AD) around the sixth century, and its meaning is less certain. There are various means and ways used to approach the ministry years of Jesus here on earth.

Two of the references are in Luke 3: 1–2 and Acts 10: 37–38, and the dates of Tiberius' reign, which are also known and familiar, are dated around 28 to 29 AD and are the start of Jesus's ministry. Another way used to approach this is a statement about the temple in John 2: 13–20. It asserts that the temple in Jerusalem was in its forty-sixth year of construction at the start of Jesus's ministry. The temple's reconstruction was started by Herod in the eighteenth year of his reign. When I went to visit the Holy Land, it was striking to note that some of these great historical buildings

Fig 1 The author in the Holy Land (Israel).

Public Ministry

In the gospels, John the Baptist's ministry is the precursor to that of Jesus's, beginning with his baptism. Jesus begins his ministry in the open side of Judea near the River Jordan.

Jesus then travelled as he preached and performed miracles, wonders, and signs, completing his ministry at the Last Supper in Jerusalem.

From start of his ministry, He appoints twelve men who later became His apostles. In the gospels of Matthew and Mark, He, despite only briefly requesting that they join him, calls four apostles. They were fishermen and immediately consented and abandoned their professions (Matthew 4: 18–22 and Mark 1: 16–20).

According to the gospel of John, the first two to be chosen by Jesus were disciples of John the Baptist. John saw the Lord Jesus and calls him the lamb of God. At that moment, the two disciples heard this and followed Jesus. The twelve Apostles, at the opening of the passage of the Sermon on the Plain, directly identifies a large group of people as disciples (Luke 6: 17).

In Luke 10: 1–16, Jesus sends out seventy of his followers as pairs to prepare towns for his visit. He instructs those sent out to accept hospitality, heal the sick, and spread the word that the kingdom of God is at hand.

Let us the try to see His ministry in stages.

The Galilean ministry starts as Jesus returns to Galilee from the Judean Desert after being tempted by the Devil. Remember that this is the same desert that David flees to when King Saul was after him and is still the same desert that John was in as he calls for repentance. Jesus preached around Galilee in Matthew 4: 18–20. His first disciples encounter him and join Him in His travels. The period includes:

- The famous Sermon on the Mount,
- The calming of the storm,
- The feeding of the 5,000, and
- Walking on water

There are numerous miracles and parables, and it eventually ends with the confession of Peter and the transfiguration.

While He travels towards Jerusalem in the Perean ministry, Jesus returns to the area where he was baptized by John about a third of the way down from the Sea of Galilee along the Jordan

John 10: 40–42: "And went away again beyond Jordan into the place where John at first baptized; and there he abode. And many resorted unto him, and said, John did no miracle: but all things that John spake of this man were true. And many believed on him there."

Finally, the ministry in Jerusalem begins with His triumphal entry into the city of Jerusalem. In all four gospels accounts of that week, Jesus drives the money changers from the temple. We are told of the story of Judas bargaining to betray him. The period culminates in the Last Supper and Jesus's farewell prayer.

Teachings, Preaching, and Miracles

There are often discussions regarding the teachings of Jesus focusing on his words and deeds. The words include several sermons as well as parables that appear in the narratives of the gospels (most narrative parables are found in the gospel of John). His deeds include the miracles and other acts performed during ministry life. In spite of the canonical gospels, there are major source listing several teachings of Christ.

John the Baptist says in John 3: 34 and John 7: 16: "My teaching is not mine but his who sent me." He repeats the same teaching in John 14: 10: "Do you not believe that I am in the Father and the Father is in me? The words that I say to you I do not speak on my own; but the Father who dwells in me does his works."

The kingdom of God is a key element of His teachings in the New Testament. He does promise inclusion in the kingdom to those who accept his message. Jesus calls people to repent from sins and turn by way of devoting themselves to God. He tells the followers to adhere strictly to Jewish law, although He is perceived by some to have broken the law. Once they asked Him what the greatest commandment was Jesus then said to them that

(Matthew 22: 37–39). One of His profound teachings includes the teaching on loving one's enemies, refraining from hatred and lust, and turning the other cheek (Matthew 5: 21–44).

In the gospels, there are about thirty parables that form onethird of Jesus's recorded teachings. They are among longer sermons and at other places in the narrative forms. These parables often contain symbolism, and normally, they relate the physical world to that of the spiritual one. As we look closely, there are common themes in these tales that include the kindness, love, tenderness, and generosity of God. There are others that set the perils of transgression. Among most of his parables, such as the Prodigal Son (Luke 15: 11–32), they are relatively simple, whilst others like the growing seed are abstruse.

In all these gospel narratives, Jesus gives a large portion of his time in ministering and performing miracles. All four accounts record at least thirty-six miracles that can be classified into two major groups: healing miracles and nature miracles.

Healing miracles included cures for physical ailments, exorcisms, and raising the dead. The nature miracle shows Jesus's power over nature (for example, turning water into wine, walking on water, calming a storm, rebuking the fig tree, and many more. Jesus teaches that His miracles are from a divine source who is God through the working of the Holy Spirit. When oppositions accused Him of performing exorcisms by the power of Beelzebub, the prince of demons, Jesus counters that he performs them by the Spirit of God (Matthew 12: 28) or finger of God (Luke 11: 20).

Furthermore, Jesus's miracles are described as signs, performed to prove his mission and work to His own people. Still, in the state, when asked to give them miraculous signs to prove his authority, He would suffer them and denied them. The gospels record the crowds regularly responding to Jesus's miracles. In the gospel of John, Jesus is presented as unpressured by the crowds, who often respond to his miracles with trust and faith. One more characteristic shared among all miracles in the gospel accounts is that He performed them freely as God gave freely the gift of life. Most of the miraculous signs and wonders teach us on the importance of faith and patience. Like in the one regarding the cleansing of ten lepers and the raising of Jairus' daughter, we are told that the healing was because of their faith.

Proclamation as Christ and Transfiguration

In the middle of each of the four gospels, there are two related episodes that mark a turning point in the narratives:

- the confession of Peter
- the transfiguration of Jesus

Both events happened near Caesarea Philippi, which was north of the Sea of Galilee, nearly at the starting of the final journey to Jerusalem that ends in the passion and His resurrection. The events mark the beginning of the disclosure of the true messianic identity of Jesus to the disciples and His prediction of His own suffering, denial by His own people, and death on the cross.

Peter's confession starts as an ongoing dialogue between Jesus and His disciples in Matthew 16: 13, Mark 8: 27, and Luke 9: 18. However, in the gospel of Matthew, we see Jesus asking His disciples the famous question, "Who do you say that I am?"

Simon answers, "You are the Messiah, the Son of the living God."

Then the Lord Jesus said to Simon Peter, "Blessed are you, Simon son of Jonah! For flesh and blood has not revealed this to you, but my Father in heaven."

The important thing here is that when Jesus affirms that the titles Peter ascribes to him are divinely revealed, thus unequivocally declaring himself to be both Christ and the Son of God.

What took place at the transfiguration appears in Matthew 17: 1–9, Mark 9: 2–8, and Luke 9: 28–36. He took Peter and two other disciples up mountain, where He was transfigured before them. The Bible tells us that His face shone like the sun, and His clothes became dazzling white.

Matthew 17: 19 says, "A bright cloud appears around them, and a voice from the cloud says, "This is my Son, the Beloved; with him I am well pleased; listen to him."

The transfiguration reconfirms that He is the Son of God. The command "listen to him" identifies Him as God's messenger and mouthpiece.

Final Week: Betrayal, Arrest, Trial, and Death

In all Christian history, writings, and poetry, when it comes to issues regarding the final week, it is an agonizing and painful part in biblical history. The last week is famously known as the Passion Week and occupies about one-third of the narrative. It begins, however, with a description of the triumphal entry into Jerusalem on the back of a colt and ends with His crucifixion.

Final Entry into Jerusalem

In all the gospels, Jesus's entry into Jerusalem takes place at the beginning of the last week of his life, just a few days before the Last Supper. This marks the beginning of the Passion narrative. The day of entry into Jerusalem is noted in Mark and John. As He left Bethany, He rides a young colt into Jerusalem.

Psalm 118: 25

Among the four gospels, only three record His entry into Jerusalem. This is followed by the cleansing of the temple when He expels the money changers from the temple. It is the only isolated moment where Jesus uses physical force in all the gospels (John 2: 13–16).

We are also told of the well-known parables and sermons, such as the widow's giving of the offering and the second coming prophecy. There is also a record of the events that took place between Jesus and the Jewish elders during Passion Week.

Last Supper

The Last Supper is meant to be the final meal that Jesus shares with his twelve disciples before His death by crucifixion. It is mentioned in all four gospels: 1 Corinthians 11: 23–26.

During that meal, Jesus predicted that one of his disciples would betray him (Matthew 26: 23–25 and John 13: 26–27). Soon, His betrayal was eminent. "Jesus answered, He it is, to whom I shall give a sop, when I have dipped it. And when he had dipped the sop, he gave it to Judas Iscariot, the son of Simon. And after the sop Satan entered into him. Then said Jesus unto him, that thou doest, do quickly."

He then goes on to predict that Simon Peter will deny him three times before the rooster crows.

In Luke 22: 34, we see also that Matthew and Mark provide descriptions of what happened after the meal (Matthew 26: 31–34 and Mark 14: 27–30). John provides the only account of Jesus washing his disciples' feet before the meal.

Agony in the Garden: Betrayal and Arrest

As they finished the Last Supper, Jesus is accompanied by His disciples as He goes to pray. Matthew and Mark speak of the place as the garden of Gethsemane, while Luke identifies it as the Mount of Olives. After His arrest, the disciples go into hiding as Peter was questioned three times. He maintains his denials about Jesus. After the third denial, he hears the rooster crow and recalls what Jesus had said to him. Peter then weeps bitterly.

Trials by the Sanhedrin, Herod, and Pilate

As He was arrested, Jesus is taken to the Sanhedrin, a Jewish judicial body. The gospel accounts differ on the details and times of the trials (Matthew 26: 57, Mark 14: 53, and Luke 22: 54). He then is taken to the house of the high priest, Caiaphas, where Jesus was mocked and beaten. John 18: 12–14 records that Jesus is first taken to Annas, the fatherin-law of Caiaphas, and then to the high priest.

At the initial trial, Jesus says little, mounts no defence, and gives very infrequent and indirect answers to the questions.

In Matthew 26: 62, Jesus's unresponsiveness leads Caiaphas to ask him, "Have you no answer?"

In Mark 14: 61, Jesus is asked, "Are you the Messiah, the Son of the Blessed One?"

Jesus replies, "I am." He follows by the saying about the coming of the Son of Man, which then provokes Caiaphas to tear his own robe in anger and accuse Jesus of blasphemy. However, there is still a major problem there as blasphemy is not punishable by death under the Roman rule, so they changed and accused Him of treason. In Matthew and Luke, Jesus's answer is more ambiguous and too general.

Matthew 26: 64 says, "You have said so." Luke 22: 70 says, "You say that I am."

As they are taking Him to Pilate, the Jewish elders, seeking a more serious punishment that will result in His death. However, the use of the word *king* is central and subtle to the discussion between Jesus and Pilate. John 18: 36 notes, "My kingdom is not from this world," but He does not unequivocally deny being the king of the Jews. Luke 23: 7–15 has Pilate realizing that Jesus was a true Galilean and that He comes under the jurisdiction of Herod Antipas.

Pilate, however, sends Jesus to Herod to be tried under Herod, but Jesus is still reluctant to say almost anything in response to questions and accusations. They mock Him and place an expensive royal robe on him to make him look like a king. They return him to Pilate, who brings the Jewish elders, telling them that Jesus has been found not guilty.

Pilate then allows a single prisoner (either Jesus or Barabbas) chosen by the crowd to be released. The elders and the mob choose to release Barabbas and crucify Jesus.

Matthew 27: 20 says, "But the chief priests and elders persuaded the multitude that they should ask Barabbas, and destroy Jesus."

In John 19: 19, Pilate writes a sign: "And Pilate wrote a title, and put it on the cross. And the writing was Jesus Of Nazareth The King Of The Jews."

The soldiers place a crown of thorns on his head and beat and taunt him before taking him to Calvary, also known as Golgotha, for crucifixion.

Crucifixion and Burial

After the trials are over, Jesus is led to Calvary carrying His cross; the route traditionally thought to have been taken is known as the Via Dolorosa. I had to go to see history in the Holy Land, and all I could do is to praise the wondrous work of the Lord.

Fig 2: The author along the Golden gates in Holy land

Three gospels identify Simon of Cyrene (a rich man) assisting him, having been compelled by the Romans to do so.

In Luke 23:27-28, Jesus tells the women in the multitude of people following him not to weep for him but for themselves and their children. At Calvary, Jesus is offered a concoction usually offered as a painkiller. Jesus is crucifies, and the solders cast lots for His clothes. Above Jesus's head on the cross is Pilate's inscription, "Jesus of Nazareth, the King of the Jews." His cross is between two convicted thieves, one of whom rebukes Jesus. The other defends him. The soldiers break the two thieves' legs (a procedure designed to hasten death in a crucifixion), but they do not break those of Jesus.

He was already dead, and it was so as to fulfil the scriptures. In John 19: 34, it says, "But one of the soldiers with a spear pierced his side, and forthwith came there out blood and water." It is not long after that that we hear the soldier's testimony that Jesus was truly the Son of God.

One of the soldiers pierces Jesus's side, and blood and water flow out (Matthew 27: 51–54). When Jesus dies, the curtain in the temple is torn from top to bottom, and an earthquake breaks open tombs. Joseph of Arimathea, with Pilate's permission and with Nicodemus' help, removes Jesus' body from the cress, wrap him in a clean cloth, and buries him in a new rock-hewn tomb

Fig 3 The author at what is believed to be the garden tomb.

In Matthew 27: 62–66, on the following day, the Jews ask Pilate for the tomb to be sealed with a stone and placed under guard to ensure the body would remain there.

Resurrection and Ascension

New Testament accounts of Jesus's resurrection tell us that on the first day of the week after the crucifixion, His tomb was discovered to be empty and His followers encountered him raised. His disciples arrived at the tomb early in the morning and met angels dressed in bright robes (Mark 16: 9 and John 20: 15). Jesus first appears to Mary Magdalene (Luke 24: 1). Jesus makes a series of appearances to the disciples (Simon Peter and Thomas) as well as Cleopas with Nicodemus on their road to Emmaus.

Before He ascends into heaven, He commissions His disciples to spread His gospel to all the nations. Luke 24: 51 says that He is then "received up into heaven." There is a better elaboration of His ascension in Acts 1: 1–11 and in 1 Timothy 3: 16. We see in Acts that forty days after the resurrection, as the disciples look on, "He was lifted up, and a cloud took him out of their sight."

1 Peter 3: 22 says, "Jesus has gone into heaven and is at the right hand of God."

We are also told in Acts of the several appearances of Jesus in visions after his ascension. In Acts 7: 55, in the vision experienced by Stephen just before his death, on the road to Damascus, Saul says, "I am Jesus, whom you are persecuting" Acts 9: 5. In Acts 9: 10–18,

Why Jesus Came To Earth

Every man's dilemma is sin. No one is exempt from this. Thanks be to God, though, who had a solution from the beginning of the world. At a certain point in time, He would become man (John 1: 14) and die for our sins (John 12: 24). Somewhere in the eons of eternity, it was decided that the son would be sent to earth. He was sent from heaven to earth to fulfil a mission of the utmost importance – to take care of man's debt of sin. He is the "Lamb slain from the foundation of the world" (Revelation 13: 8b).

He came to seek those who are lost (Matthew 18: 11 and Luke 9: 56 and 19: 10).

Jesus's coming to earth is described in: Philippians 2: 6. This is the reason he became a man: to give His body as a sacrifice for our sin. He became human to save sinful humanity. From the beginning, required was a substitutionary sacrifice for our sin. In the Old Testament, sacrifice of animals was only a temporary means to cover sin, so it was necessary to have something more, more powerful, and longer lasting. Jesus is not just a human atoning for all the sins; He is God come in human flesh.

1 Timothy 3: 16. "And without controversy great is the mystery of godliness: God was manifest in the flesh,

justified in the Spirit, seen of angels, preached unto the Gentiles, believed on in the world, received up into glory."

He died once for all and took the sin of the world. Unlike the Old Testament sacrifices that could never take away sins and needed to be repeated, with Jesus's death, it had to be done once and for all. As God, the His death had infinite value and His priesthood is an eternal one because the one who died was an eternal being (Hebrews 9: 12–15, Hebrews 5: 9 and 9: 26, and 1 Peter 1: 20).

"He then would have had to suffer often since the foundation of the world; but now, once at the end of the ages, He has appeared to put away sin by the sacrifice of Himself."

Jesus came at a time when the Jewish culture was collapsing under the burdens of the Pharisees and oppression by the Romans taxes and practices. The Jews place their belief pattern upon the Law of Moses and an additional hundred-plus laws for every one of the 613. It was a time of spiritual corruption where the people no longer knew the truth. Eventually, as a result, they were brought under the leadership of those who claimed to know the truth but actually led them away from it. Jesus said to them in John 8: 32, "And you shall know the truth, and the truth shall make you free."

Verse 36 says, "Therefore if the Son makes you free, you shall be free indeed."

Paul, who personally experienced this freedom, said, "But now having been set free from sin, and having become slaves of God, you have your fruit to holiness, and the end, everlasting life" (Romans 6: 22).

Jesus continued to give His disciples more information about His purpose for coming to earth (Mark 8: 31 and John 12: 23–25).

It is explained what Jesus said before He came to earth in Hebrews 10: 5–10. Once and for all, everything spoken of that related to sin in the Old Testament was taken care of. Jesus came to set everyone free from their own spiritual oppression, sin that brought bondage to those who were religious and those who are not.

Paul wrote, "This is a faithful saying and worthy of all acceptance, that Christ Jesus came into the world to save sinners, of whom I am chief" (1 Timothy 1: 15).

As knowledgeable as Paul was, Paul understood God so loved the world that He sent his Son (Romans 5: 8).

Jesus explains in John 10: 11 that, "I am the good shepherd. The good shepherd gives His life for the sheep."

This was God's plan (Acts 2: 23–25): Jesus was brought back to life in the very same body He was sacrificed in. He went to heaven to sit at the right hand of God (Romans 8: 34).

Ephesians 1: 19–20. This is why there is no one greater than Jesus, who is the Saviour of all mankind. In John 8: 20–24, He told those who disbelieve who He said He will die in their sin but He offered them life. He offers you life today as well. 2 Corinthians 4: 4 is about God becoming man. There is no salvation if you do not believe the Gospel message. If Jesus is anything but the eternal God in flesh, you have not the Jesus of history or the Bible. You must believe the Bible. It teaches the deity of Christ to be saved. It's not your or my opinion of Jesus. Rather, it is what God says in His word about the Son. If you do not have the same testimony, you have nothing.

"The first man was of the earth, made of dust; the second Man is the Lord from heaven" (1 Corinthians 15: 47).

The first man, Adam, was made supernaturally from the earth. The second man, whom the Bible calls the last Adam, was also brought into this world supernaturally by a virgin conceiving.

In Luke 2: 10–12, it says, "Then the angel said to them, "Do not be afraid, for behold, I bring you good tidings of great joy which will be to all people. "For there is born to you this day in the city of David a Savior, who is Christ the Lord. "And this will be the sign to you: You will find a Babe wrapped in swaddling clothes, lying in a manger."

"It pleased God through the foolishness of the message preached to save those who believe" (1 Corinthians 1: 21).

If salvation came by any work that we could do, then Jesus did not need to be our Saviour. We could be our own saviours. But there is nothing that we do, no matter how great, that is acceptable to God for salvation. He accepts only His Son's work and those who place faith in the message.

John 12: 44 says, "Then Jesus cried out and said, "He who believes in Me, believes not in Me but in Him who sent Me."

Many have made God by their own concept. They claim to believe in Him, but if you do not believe in Jesus, you do not believe in God. No matter what religious persuasion one adheres to (even Judaism), He made it clear that you do not believe in the Father (God) who sent Him to earth to represent Him.

At one point in the ministry of Jesus, Thomas said to Jesus, "we don't know the way. Jesus said- I AM THE WAY" (John 14: 5–6). Jesus is showing that He is exclusive – that people who do not follow him can be excluded. To be included, one must make a choice. Those who see Him for who He is accept His sacrifice.

"And this is the promise that He has promised us-- eternal life. These things I have written to you concerning those who try to deceive you." (1 John 2: 25–26). There is only one way to have peace and a relationship with the God of the universe. God himself has made the way to come to

Him: "And this is the testimony: that God has given us eternal life, and this life is in His Son. He who has the Son has life; he who does not have the Son of God does not have life" (1 John 5: 11–12).

God's gift to the world is His Son. It is His personal gift to you, but to unwrap it, you need faith to believe and receive the message. It is a life-changing offer. Who of us does not need a new start on life?

Attitude toward Life

- Let go of the assumption that the world is against you or that you were born with a grey cloud over your head. It is an assumption that has no basis in reason or science. The sooner you can attribute your pessimism to a unique set of circumstances rather than the state of the world itself, the easier it will be to change your perspective.
- Understand that the past does not equal the future. Just because you have experienced pain or disappointment in the past does not guarantee that everything else that starts badly will end badly. Do not make a bad start turn into a self-fulfilling prophecy for a bad ending.
- See yourself as a cause, not an effect. You do not have to be a product or a victim of your circumstances. Stop thinking about what is happening to you, and start thinking about what you can make happen. If you are not happy with the way your life is now, set goals and get moving. Use your negative experiences to build

character and make better decisions. Life involves taking many risks every day, and not all of them will end positively. That's what defines risk. But the flip side is that some actions will lead to good results, and it is generally better to have a mixed bag than to have nothing at all. Ideally, the good stuff will outweigh the bad, but you never reach that point unless you put yourself out there.

• Use positive affirmations. Write down short statements that remind you of what you are trying to change about the way you see the world. Put them in places where you'll see them every day, such as on your bathroom mirror, the inside of your locker, on your computer monitor, or even taped to your shower wall. Some affirmations to start with are: "Anything is possible," "My circumstances do

not create me, I create my circumstances," "The only thing I can control is my attitude towards life," "I always have a choice," and "I choose to live the positive side of life."

• Remember that life is short. When you feel pessimism clouding your judgment or you start to feel down about the future, remind yourself that every minute counts. Any time spent brooding guarantees nothing but less time to enjoy whatever life might have to offer. At its core, pessimism is impractical because it causes you to spend time dwelling on things that have not yet happened and aren't guaranteed to happen, and it prevents you from getting things done. Pessimism breeds indecision. It's a waste of time, and time is a limited resource that you cannot afford to take for granted.

- Finally, be a balanced optimist. Nobody is suggesting that you become an oblivious Pollyanna, pretending that nothing bad can or ever will happen. Doing so can lead to poor decisions and invites people to take advantage of you. Instead, be a rational optimist who takes the good with the bad in hopes of the good ultimately outweighing the bad and with the understanding that being pessimistic about everything accomplishes nothing. Prepare for the worst, but hope for the best. The former makes you sensible, and the latter makes you an optimist.

Tips

- Use quotes to remind yourself how to be optimistic. Remember sayings like, "Even the longest journey begins with a single step," "Life has a way of reminding one that it can be worse," "Until one understands the low and darker side of life, the appreciation of the awe-inspiring highs will remain stagnant," and "Every cloud has a silver lining."
- Look happy. Studies have shown that putting a positive expression on your face can actually make you feel happier and more optimistic about the future.

- Practice by conveying these ideas to others. If someone is being pessimistic, talk about changing negative attitudes. Sometimes, it is easier to understand a perspective if you have to explain it to others.
- No matter how odd this may sound, listen to optimistic music (that you like) and read books that have at least a little optimism in them. Avoid cynical/pessimistic entertainment: You are what you watch.
- Pass a blessing on to a friend or stranger – let somebody have that parking space and let somebody in front of you in line at the market. Doing nice things for others is an instant positive pick-me-up.
- Only you can make the situation better, so smile and make the situation better. Count your blessings, each and every little one. Focusing on the good things in your life, no matter how small or seemingly insignificant will help frame a better attitude and take your mind off of the negatives.
- Try to avoid negative people. If you can't avoid them, learn how to not let them get you down. Everyone has their times of weakness. You may stumble at times and fall into bad habits, but never give up. Gradually, you will succeed.
- Don't confuse pessimism with depression. Depression can make everything look worse than it is. If you are depressed, seek help.

- While it is true that you create your own circumstances, accept that the past is the past. Do not let negative circumstances trigger irrational guilt or pessimism.
- Realize that it is not about what happens to you. Rather, it is about how you react to what happens.

Negative Thinking

Negative attitudes come from negative thoughts that come from reactions to negative behaviour. And around the cycle goes. We know that none of this negative stuff is coming from God. There is nothing negative about the way He thinks or acts. So how do we put a stop to all this nonsense? How do we get to a place where our positive attitude is what is natural for us and not the other way around? I wish I could give you a magic formula that, when applied correctly, would erase your negative attitude in three days. But, alas, the real world isn't quite so simple. The good news is that there are some things we can do to help transition from the land of negativity to a much more positive place by trusting the Word of God.

Positive Thinking Tips for a Positive Attitude

Thinking starts with thoughts. The mind is an empty shell without thoughts. The human mind is precious. It is the centre where thoughts are developed into imaginations for good things or bad. It is in our minds that decisions are made and processed into actions. An empty mind is not good. An evil mind is unprofitable too. An idle mind is equally not beneficial because there is no growth nor movement. Below are tips on how we can successfully utilize our mind to receive maximum benefits as well as how we can guard the mind. The mind also is a battle ground where victory or failure emanates from.

- **Focus on what you're thinking about.** Remember what I said about being stuck because we never addressed the source? Our negative actions and words are coming from our negative thoughts. Our body, including the mouth, has no choice but to follow wherever our mind goes. We can control our thoughts, regardless of what we have been led to believe. As soon as a negative thought comes into your mind, purposefully make it a point to replace it with a positive one. 2 Corinthians 10: 5 says you are to remain positive to correct good thoughts. Dwell on things that are good and lovely which are more desired (Philippians 4: 8). Put away unnecessary thoughts and unfruitful elements.

- **Stop letting other people's negative attitudes influence change you.** Stop hanging around with people who do nothing but spout negative stuff. In one of my sermons, I was teaching that three things should change in a person's life in order to see new things and enjoy permanent change. Change your associates, change your education, and change your socialization. By doing this, bad things will be traditionally dropped.

We cannot afford to do this when our goal is to become more positive. The negative people in our life are not going to like it, but they should go.

- **Make a list of all the areas in your life that you want to change**. If you can't think of things to put on your list, just ask an honest friend and not a critic.

- **Take some time to write strong, life-giving, positive affirmation statements.** Read those statements out loud every day. Enjoy how great they make you feel. Read Bible stories that are uplifting, and make progress by remaining on the right and positive track, even if you can't see it just yet. Just keep affirming and confessing positive words and attitudes as often as you can.

- **Take time to pray about this.** You cannot change by yourself. But you can spend time with the One who is able to help. Do what you can, and let God do the rest. It really is that simple.

This process will change how we think, and that is the real key to changing how we act. Remember, the body will follow wherever the mind goes. There is no way to separate the two, so we might as well program in what we want instead of leaving it to chance. Just know that God's version of a right attitude contains nothing negative. If we want God's best for our life, it starts with right thoughts — His thoughts, to be exact.

The Tongue

The things we say have power. God tells us what He did with our tongues. He says, "I have put life and death on your tongue." However, it is our ultimate choice to choose the right thing. Proverbs 18: 21 says, "Death and life are in the power of the tongue, and those who love it will eat its fruit."

God has trusted us to the point that He trusts you to make good independent decisions and choices for short and long term. However, as we are free in making these choices, we ought to be responsible for the choices that we make. Moreover, we fashion our surroundings by how and what we say and do. The manner in how we speak can bring us friends, war, trust, peace, or hatred. The gossiper did not suddenly appear from nowhere. Rather, he was born from what his tongue says. We have been trained to much listen more than talk. Talking can also bring us to God or away from God. Learning to talk and to hear have been neglected subjects for quite some time. Your tongue is vital. The words of your mouth should be filled with wisdom. David says in Psalm 19: 14, "I have realised that the more we talk the more we can be reckless with words."

The Power of Your Tongue

There came a time in history of the children of Israel when God would come down to hear what they are saying.

Numbers 14: 28

There is a force and ability to create that is within our lips. The laws we have in the Bible came from what God was saying. His words became "my law," says David. In Genesis, God spoke the word, and out of His speaking, all we see today came into existence. He spoke forth and created this world. There is a good lesson to learn here. As much as you are tired of the things around, you try to change the way you use your tongue. Positive fulfilment is a by-product of your tongue. The same goes with thinking you are not how you think about yourself. As "a man thinkest in his heart, so is he". Similarly, as in the manner of you are talking, so are you. Salvation is never complete without the use of your tongue,

Romans 10: 9 says, "With the heart a man believes unto salvation." That is true, but believing without using your tongue cannot complete the great mystery of salvation. "With your mouth you have to confess," which again we see the employment of the tongue. Positive use of the tongue brings positive rewards. I have seen people go into prison and spend many years because of how they used their tongues. Reckless use brings problems and consequences that are rife. There are also those who are hated by many because they say anything to the extent of saying things that cannot be established as correct. Start with positive thinking, and you will also see and experience sweet and positive talk. You will never know a fool until he opens his mouth at taste the fruit of his tongue. The proper and wise use of the tongue has set ordinary man on thrones and some as presidents. You can never know a fool until he opens his mouth. You are maybe down there because you have not made a choice of disciplining your tongue into positive confession of who you really God created to be. In the book of Joshua, we learn that only those among the children of Israel who spoke well about themselves were able to stand against their enemies. Your tongue can bring you fear and henceforth defeat. Intimidation did send Saul and the host of Israel into hiding while Goliath was on high use of his tongue. The truth of the matter was that Goliath did not kill anyone from the camp of Israel. All he was able to do was use his tongue until a positive tongue came to challenge and slew him. This is the same with the Devil who told you that you are going to die poor and barren, that your sickness has no cure, that you will never own your own house, and so forth. These are the words the Devil spoke, but we came against them in the name of Jesus Christ. God did not create you to suffer and die poor; it is a lie from the Devil. Speak victory all the time, and it will be yours. Be inspired to think right and to positively talk big and well about yourself. Do you know that it is hard to speak well of other people when you do not speak well of yourself? Today, look generally at the appearance of a gossiper in your community and make a close analysis. You will see that even their dressing is lacking and the kind of car they drive is not so great.

What Should You Know about the Tongue?

At the end of our lives here on earth, we shall all give an account on every idle word we spoke. Matthew 12: 36 says it is important to note that you cannot rise beyond the level of your words. The inherent power of words is so amazing. There is strength in words to bind, to loosen, to enslave, or to set free. Look below at what words can do.

Words can bless, curse, love, hurt, offend, shun, blasphemy, or provoke.

In the Word of God, Jesus taught us about the rich man (Luke 16: 19–31). As I was reading, I noted that the only pain the rich man had was on the tongue and the drop of water he wanted from Lazarus was only for his tongue. Human problems emanate from the tongue and from foolish thoughts, and I would like to call it the tongue trouble. Your battle should be to match what you say with the Word of God. In James 3: 5–11, it says that even though the tongue is a little member of the body, we bless God and we curse people who are in the image of God (similitude of God) with the same tongue. The deception here is on this foolishness; do not use the same tongue you use to bless and worship God to curse your neighbour.

This should not happen (Proverbs 15: 1 and 18: 21, Psalm 34: 13, and Matthew 12: 34).

Let us examine how we talk negatively about ourselves regarding circumstances in comparison with the Word of God.

WHAT YOU USUALLY SAY	WHAT GOD SAY
My situation is impossible	**Mark 10:27** But Jesus looked at them and said, "With men *it is* impossible, but not with God; for with God all things are possible." **Luke 18:27** But He said, "The things which are impossible with men are possible with God."
I am too tired now	**Matthew 11:28** Come to Me, all *you* who labor and are heavy laden, and I will give you rest.
Nobody loves me	**John 3:16** For God so loved the world that He gave His only begotten Son, that whoever believes in Him should not perish but have everlasting life.

I cannot go on	**2 Corinthians 12:9** And He said to me, "My grace is sufficient for you, for My strength is made perfect in weakness." Therefore most gladly I will rather boast in my infirmities, that the power of Christ may rest upon me.
I cannot figure out things	**Proverbs 3:5-6** Trust in the LORD with all your heart, And lean not on your own understanding; In all your ways acknowledge Him, And He shall direct your paths.
I cannot do it	**Philippians 4:13** I can do all things through Christ who strengthens me
I cannot forgive myself	**1 John 1:9** If we confess our sins, He is faithful and just to forgive us *our* sins and to cleanse us from all unrighteousness.
It is not worth it	**Romans 8:28** And we know that all things work together for good to those who love God, to those who are the called according to *His* purpose.

I cannot manage with this little	**Philippians 4:19** And my God shall supply all your need according to His riches in glory by Christ Jesus.
I am always worried and frustrated	**1 Peter 5:7** casting all your care upon Him, for He cares for you
I am afraid	**2 Timothy 1:7** For God has not given us a spirit of fear, but of power and of love and of a sound mind.
I do not have enough faith	**Romans 12:3** For I say, through the grace given to me, to everyone who is among you, not to think *of himself* more highly than he ought to think, but to think soberly, as God has dealt to each one a measure of faith
I am no smart enough	**1 Corinthians 1:30** But of Him you are in Christ Jesus, who became for us wisdom from God—and righteousness and sanctification and redemption
I am so lonely	**Hebrews 13:5** *Let your* conduct *be* without covetousness; *be* content with

	such things as you have. For He Himself has said, "I will never leave you nor forsake you

Psalm 45: 1 says, "My heart is overflowing with a good theme; I recite my composition concerning the King;"

My tongue is the pen of a ready writer. When you say words, you are actually writing them on your heart.

Positive Confession

Say the following to yourself:

"I am who God says I am, and I can do what God says I can do in the name of Jesus. No sickness, disease, plague, illness, or infirmity will come near me or my dwellings because greater is he that is in me than he that is in the world."

1 John 4: 4: "you are of God, little children, and have overcome them, because He who is in you is greater than he who is in the world. By his stripes I am healed"

Isaiah 53: 5: "But He was wounded for our transgressions, He was bruised for our iniquities; the chastisement for our peace was upon Him, and by His stripes we are healed."

Isaiah 54: 17: "No weapon formed against you shall prosper, and every tongue which rises against you in judgment you shall condemn. This is the heritage of the servants of the Lord, and their righteousness is from Me," Says the Lord. I am the head and not the tail, I am above and not beneath";

Deuteronomy 28: 13: "And the Lord will make you the head and not the tail; you shall be above only, and not be beneath, if you heed the commandments of the Lord your God, which I command you today, and are careful to observe them."

Psalm 23: "The Lord is my shepherd; I shall not want."

Philippians 4: 19: "and my God shall supply all your need according to His riches in glory by Christ Jesus."

I am successful, I am prosperous, and all my promises are made and are achievable in Jesus name.

Praise God.

Reflections/ Notes:

Glossary

- **Agape:** The God kind of love.
- **Allegory:** This is a representation of one thing which is intended to excite the representation of another event, thing or story.
- **Alpha:** The beginning
- **Anoint:** To rub oil on, smear, or set apart as in consecrate for holy use.
- **Apostasy:** To rebel from correct doctrine, falling away from that which is sound teaching or doctrine; un-doctrinate.
- **Atonement:** The act of making amends – to repair a wrong done against God.
- **Attributes:** The attributes of God are specific characteristics of God discussed in Christian theology.
- **Barabbas:** The son of Abba, father, a notorious robber whom Pilate proposed to condemn to death instead of Jesus, whom he wished to release.
- **Canon:** A rule used to measure authenticity of a scripture.
- **Christology:** Relating to the person, nature, and personification of Christ.
- **Discernment:** Ability to use spiritual judgment.

- **Ecclesiastes:** A book of the Tanakh (Bible) classified as one of the Ketuvim.
- **Emancipate:** To set free from oppression.

- **Hope:** Firm, confident expectation in God where there is firm assurance.
- **Glorified:** Describe or represent as admirable, elevate, dignify, or honour.
- **Impute:** To ascribe to someone righteous by virtue of similar qualities of another person.
- **Justified:** Being declared or being made righteous before a holy God.
- **Prominence:** State of being important, noticeable, valued, prestigious in nature.
- **Redeemer:** One who takes another from danger to safety.
- **Restitution:** An act of restoring back to the owner something that had been lost or stolen away.
- **Resurrection:** A state of being brought back to life after encountering death.
- **Revelation:** Divine enlightenment by way of revealing a mystery.
- **Saints:** A name used to refer to the followers of Christian faith (in a church).
- **Sanctified:** Literally meaning to make holy – to set holy by consecrating

- **Worship:** To ascribe worthiness by subjecting oneself to God by extoling high.

Bible Study Scriptures

Isaiah 53: 5: "but he was wounded for our transgressions, he was bruised for our iniquities: the chastisement of our peace was upon him; and with his stripes we are healed."

Mark 9: 23: "Jesus said unto him, if thou canst believe, all things are possible to him that believeth."

Romans 10: 17: "So then faith cometh by hearing, and hearing by the Word of God."

Acts 1: 9–11: "and when he had spoken these things, while they beheld, he was taken up; and a cloud received him out of their sight. And while they looked stedfastly toward heaven as he went up, behold, two men stood by them in white apparel; which also said, Ye men of Galilee, why stand ye gazing up into heaven? This same Jesus, which is taken up from you into heaven, shall so come in like manner as ye have seen him go into heaven"

John 10: 10: "the thief cometh not, but for to steal, and to kill, and to destroy: I am come that they might have life, and that they might have it more abundantly"

John 1: 1: "in the beginning was the Word, and the Word was with God, and the Word was God **Verse 12** but as many as received him, to them gave he power to become the sons of God, even to them that believe on his name: **Verse 14** And the Word was made flesh, and dwelt among us, (and we beheld his glory, the glory as of the only begotten of the Father,) full of grace and truth."

John 1: 1: "and verse 14 Jesus gives us a chance to allow Him and His Father to come and dwell in us."

Revelation 3: 20-21: "Behold, I stand at the door, and knock: if any man hear my voice, and open the door, I will come into him, and will sup with him, and he with me. To him that overcometh will I grant to sit with me in my throne, even as I also overcame, and am set down with my Father in his throne?"

2 Corinthians 5: 17: "Therefore if any man be in Christ, he is a new creature: old things are passed away; behold all things are become new."

Colossians 1: 26-27: "Even the mystery which hath been hid from ages and from generations, but now is made manifest to his saints: to whom God would make known what is the riches of the glory of this mystery among the Gentiles; which is Christ in you, the hope of glory."

John 8: 32: "And ye shall know the truth, and the truth shall make you free."

Proverbs 23: 7: "for as he thinketh in his heart, so is he: Eat and drink, saith he to thee; but his heart is not with thee."

Philippians 2: 12: "Wherefore, my beloved, as ye have always obeyed, not as in my presence only, but now much more in my absence, work out your own salvation with fear and trembling."

Romans 7: 21-25: "I find then a law, that, when I would do good, evil is present with me. For I delight in the law of God after the inward man: But I see another law in my members, warring against the law of my mind, and bringing me into captivity to the law of sin which is in my members. O wretched man that I am! Who shall deliver me from the body of this death? I thank God through Jesus Christ our Lord. So then with the mind I myself serve the law of God; but with the flesh the law of sin."

1 Corinthians 9: 27: "but I keep under my body, and bring it into subjection: lest that by any means, when I have preached to others, I myself should be a castaway."

Genesis 1: 27: "So God created man in his own image, in the image of God created he him; male and female created he them."

Romans 5: 12: "wherefore, as by one man sin entered into the world and death by sin; and so death passed upon all men, for that all have sinned:"

All scriptures and direct and indirect quotations are taken from the Holy Bible, which we have received and accepted as the only authority in Christian faith. Quoted are scriptures from the King James Version, the New King James Version, the New International Version, and the American Standard Version.

Scripture quotation marked KJV are from the Holy Bible, King James Version (Authorized Version). First published in 1611. Quoted from the KJV Classic Reference Bible. Copyright ©1983 by The Zondervan Corporation.

Scripture quotations marked NKJV are taken from the New King James Version. Copyright ©1982 by Thomas Nelson, Inc. Used by Permission. All rights reserved.

Scripture Quotations NIV are taken from the Holy Bible. New International Version®. NIV®. Copyright © 1973,

Additional resources include:

Landau, Sidney. Dictionaries: The Art and Craft of Lexicography (ed 2). *2nd Ed.* Cambridge: Cambridge University Press, 2001.

Charlesworth, James H. Jesus and Archaeology. Grand Rapids, Michigan: Wm. B. Eerdmans Publishing, 2006.

We would love to hear from you, Get in contact with us; send your comments and testimonial to:

E-mail: nomusa@nomusabuleni.co.uk

Phone: +447878178 473

Inspirations of life in faith

Inspirationsoflifeinfaith

Nomusa buleni

nomusa_buleni

www.nomusabuleni.co.uk

Nomusa Buleni